THE TIMES
PICTURE COLLECTION
EXPLORERS

THE TIMES
PICTURE COLLECTION
EXPLORERS

Richard Sale
and
Madeleine Lewis

Collins

An Imprint of HarperCollinsPublishers

ISBN-10:0–00–714566–7
ISBN-13:978–0–00–714566–9

ISBN-10:0–06–081905–7 (in the United States)
ISBN-13:978–0–06–081905–7

FIRST U.S. EDITION: HarperCollins books may be purchased for educational, business, or sales promotional use. For information in the United States, please write to: Special Markets Department, HarperCollins Publishers, 10 East 53rd Street, New York, NY 10022.

Designed by Colin Brown

Printed and bound in Italy by Editoriale Johnson

05 06 07 08 09
9 8 7 6 5 4 3 2 1

The publishers would like to thank: Sue Lawford, Alpine Club Photo Library; Pauline Hubner and Justin Hobson, Royal Geographical Society; Dick Bass; Lucy Martin, Scott Polar Research Institute; Erik Decamp; and particular thanks to Amanda Faber for all her work in the development stage of the project.

PICTURE CREDITS

All reasonable efforts have been made by the Publisher to trace the copyright holders of the photographs contained in this publication. In the event that a copyright holder of a photograph has not been traced, but comes forward after the publication of this edition, the Publishers will endeavour to rectify the position at the earliest opportunity. The Publishers are grateful to the following individuals and organisations for permission to reproduce their photographs.

2–3 RGS **5–9** Richard Sale **10** TNL **10–11** Scott Polar Research Institute, University of Cambridge **12** (top) National Maritime Museum, London (bottom) RGS **13** (top) Popperfoto (bottom) Richard Sale **14** (top) RGS (bottom) Richard Sale Collection **15** (top) RGS (bottom) Richard Sale Collection **16** Richard Sale **17** (top) Richard Sale Collection (middle & bottom) Fred Goldberg **18** (top) Susan Barr (bottom) Hulton Archive **19** (both) Arctic and Antarctic Museum, St Petersburg **20** Richard Sale Collection **20–21** Richard Sale **21** (right) Richard Sale Collection **22** RGS **23** Hulton Archive **24** (both) Danish Polar Centre **25** (top) Rune Gjeldnes/Torry Larsen (bottom) Per Michelsen **26** (top) Arctic and Antarctic Museum, St Petersburg (bottom) Richard Sale **27** (left) Richard Sale Collection (right) Chauncey Loomis **28** Richard Sale Collection **29** (top) Hulton Archive (bottom) Richard Sale Collection **30** Corbis **31** Swedish Polar Research Secretariat **32** Richard Sale Collection **33** Per Michelsen **34** (top) Richard Sale Collection (bottom) Byrd Polar Research Centre **35** (top) Hulton Archive (bottom) Richard Sale Collection **36** (left) Richard Sale Collection (right) Bettmann/Corbis **37** (top left & right) Swedish Polar Research Secretariat (bottom) Arctic and Antarctic Museum, St Petersburg **38** Børge Ousland **39** Canterbury Museum, New Zealand **40** Richard Sale Collection **41** (top) Richard Sale Collection (bottom) Canterbury Museum, New Zealand **42** (top) RGS (bottom) Scott Polar Research Institute, University of Cambridge **43** Mansell Collection/Timepix **44** (top) Swedish Polar Research Secretariat (bottom) Scott Polar Research Institute, University of Cambridge **45** (top) Hulton Archive (bottom) Richard Sale Collection **46** Richard Sale Collection **47** Hulton Archive **48** (top) Richard Sale Collection (bottom) Scott Polar Research Institute, University of Cambridge **49–50** S.A. Museum, South Australia **51** (both) Mitchell Library, State Library of New South Wales **52** (top) RGS (bottom) Richard Sale Collection **53** (top) Richard Sale Collection (bottom) New Zealand High Commission **54** (top) Canterbury Museum, New Zealand (bottom) TNL **55** Børge Ousland **56–57** Richard Sale **58** Corbis **59–60** Richard Sale Collection **61** (left) Topham Picturepoint (right) Richard Sale **62** Mountain Camera Archive **63** Richard Sale **64** Popperfoto **65** (left) Alpine Club Photo Library, London (right) Erik Decamp **66** John Cleare **67** John McDonald **68** John Cleare/Mountain Camera **69** Alpine Club Photo Library, London **70** Richard Sale Collection **71** (left) Richard Sale Collection (right) John Cleare/Mountain Camera **72–73** Colin Monteath/Mountain Camera **74** (left) Alpine Club Photo Library, London (right) RGS **75** (left) Richard Sale Collection (right) RGS **76** RGS **77** (top) RGS (bottom) Richard Sale Collection **78** (bottom) TNL **78–79** RGS **79** (bottom) TNL **80** TNL **81** RGS **82** Louis Lachenal **83** RGS **84** Richard Sale Collection **85** Hermann Buhl **86–87** Richard Sale Collection **88** TNL **89** Fritz Wintersteller **90** (top) TNL (bottom) Richard Sale **91** Hulton Archive **92** Dick Bass **93** David Hamilton/Mountain Camera **94** (both) Richard Sale **95** Byrd Polar Research Centre **96** Richard Sale Collection **97** John Cleare/Mountain Camera **98** David Hamilton/Mountain Camera **99** Colin Monteath/Mountain Camera **100** J Ramón Agirre **101** David Scott-Macnab/Mountain Camera **102–103** Sir Wilfred Thesiger/Pitt Rivers Museum, University of Oxford, permission granted courtesy of Curtis Brown **104** Hulton-Deutsch Collection/Corbis **105–106** RGS **107** (top) RGS (bottom left) Nigel Bean/naturepl.com (bottom right) John Sparks/naturepl.com **108–109** RGS **110** Mansell Collection/TimePix **111** (both) RGS **112–113** The British Library **114** Topham Picturepoint **115–116** RGS **117** (top) RGS (bottom) Hulton Archive **118** Hulton Archive **119** RGS **120** Sir Wilfred Thesiger/Pitt Rivers Museum, University of Oxford, permission granted courtesy of Curtis Brown **121** (both) TNL **122** RGS **123** Popperfoto **124** Sir Wilfred Thesiger/Pitt Rivers Museum, University of Oxford, permission granted courtesy of Curtis Brown **125–128** RGS **129** National Library of Australia **130** State Library of South Australia **131** National Library of Australia **132–133** RGS **134–135** Loren McIntyre **136–137** Hulton-Deutsch Collection/Corbis **138** RGS **139** (top) Popperfoto/Alan Greeley (bottom) by permission of Ray Hoole, great grandson of the photographer, Francis Harold Watson **140** (above) RGS (bottom) Hulton-Deutsch Collection/Corbis **141** Bath Royal Literary and Scientific Institution **142** Mansell Collection/TimePix **143** (left) Hulton Archive (right) Bettmann/Corbis **144** (left) Hulton Archive **144–145** RGS **146** (top) Bruce Davidson/naturepl.com (bottom) Hulton-Deutsch Collection/Corbis **147** (left) TNL (right) RGS **148** (top) RGS (bottom) Topham Picturepoint **149** (top) Mansell Collection/TimePix (centre, left) Bettmann/Corbis (centre, right) Hulton-Deutsch Collection/Corbis (bottom) Brown Brothers, Sterling, PA **150** (top) TNL (bottom) RGS **151** (top) TNL (bottom) Hulton-Deutsch Collection/Corbis **152** Anthony Fiala/National Geographic Image Collection **153** (left) Anthony Fiala/National Geographic Image Collection (right) RGS **154** (top left) RGS (top right) TNL (bottom) Hiram Bingham/National Geographic Image Collection **155** (top) Hiram Bingham/National Geographic Image Collection (left) Brown Brothers, Sterling, PA (right) South American Pictures/Tony Morrison **156–157** Corbis **158** Brown Brothers, Sterling, PA **159** D.H. Clarke/PPL **160** Barry Pickthall/PPL **161** Popperfoto **162** Topham Picturepoint **163–164** Popperfoto **165** (both) Associated Press **166** (left) Pelletier Micheline/Corbis Sygma (right) Flyer/PPL **167** (left) Popperfoto (right) Topham Picturepoint **168** (top) Popperfoto (bottom) Associated Press **169** Popperfoto **170** (both) Hulton Archive **171** (top) Tom Mclean Enterprises/PPL (centre) Popperfoto (bottom) Corbis **172** (top) Popperfoto (bottom) Associated Press **173** (top) Bettmann/Corbis (bottom) Associated Press **174–181** Chris Howes/Wild Places **182** (both) Bettmann/Corbis **183** Popperfoto **184** (both) Bettmann/Corbis **185** Hulton Archive **186–187** Popperfoto **front cover** Mawson Antarctic Collection, S.A. Museum **back cover** RGS

RGS = Royal Geographical Society, London
TNL = Times Newspapers Ltd

CONTENTS

Introduction

Man's early exploration of the world was carried out not to increase his knowledge of it, but to settle it, as population pressure forced people to migrate. Only slowly, over many thousands of years, did this change. Trade came to dominate in areas where the settled population represented a formidable challenge, whilst a thirst for plunder drove explorers to regions where more vulnerable civilisations were found. The impetus behind these journeys came from the kingdoms of Europe – although the Chinese had ocean-going junks, they abandoned long-distance seafaring in the late 15th century. As was said of the Portuguese, who under Dom Enrique (Henry the Navigator to the English-speaking world) began the great voyages of exploration, 'God gave them a small country as a cradle, but an entire world as a grave'.

The Spaniards, British, Dutch and others who followed the Portuguese may have been financed by kings and merchants driven by greed, but for some of the ordinary sailors on the ships, experiencing the hardships and dangers of medieval travel, but returning again and again to the sea, there was something more profound at work. For them exploration was an end in itself, challenge and discovery being as important as reward. They were the forerunners of the explorers to whom this book is dedicated, those who sought out untouched wildernesses – mountains, the poles, jungles, deserts and the worlds beneath the ground and sea – for the joy of doing so. Many then and now question why men do such foolhardy things. To answer that question would require a book of its own, but it is worth noting the words of Fridtjof Nansen, the foremost polar explorer of his generation, whose words apply equally to all those mentioned in the following pages:

'People, perhaps, still exist who believe that it is of no importance to explore the unknown polar regions. This, of course, shows ignorance. It is hardly necessary to mention here of what scientific importance it is that these regions should be thoroughly explored. The history of the human race is a continual struggle from darkness towards light. It is, therefore, to no purpose to discuss the use of knowledge: man wants to know, and when he ceases to do so, he is no longer man.'

Richard Sale, December 2002

Ice

Of the world's ice-bound territories, the Arctic was first settled thousands of years ago by Asiatic nomads moving north, then east across the Bering Sea land bridge which connected Asia and North America during the Ice Ages. Later, from the ninth century AD, came the Vikings. They were settlers, exploring the land in order to probe its assets, to weigh up its potential to support their families. The first people to map the Arctic came from northern Europe, just as the Vikings had. They were not driven by a search for land to settle, but by the commercial requirement to find an alternative route to the riches of the Orient, since by the 15th century the Spaniards and Portuguese were in control of the Atlantic.

From Britain came John Cabot, sailing north-westwards in May 1497, to be followed years later by Frobisher, Hudson and Baffin. In 1619, the Dane Jens Munk overwintered on the eastern shore of Hudson Bay, he and two others being the only survivors of a 65-man expedition. Later (in 1631),Thomas James was forced to overwinter in what is now James Bay: his book on the journey is widely believed to have inspired Coleridge to write *The Rime of the Ancient Mariner*.

By contrast to the Arctic, the Antarctic was discovered not by mapping the land, but by probing the ocean and so mapping where there was no land. In the north, men had expected to find ocean and in fact found land: in the south they expected to find a continent and saw only water. In 1642 the Dutchman Abel Tasman sailed around Australia, proving it was not part of a southern continent, and in the years that followed expeditions beyond latitude 50°S showed that the Southern Ocean was an empty place, pushing back the possible shores of the expected land mass. In 1578 Englishman Francis Drake was blown south to about 57°S, while another Englishman, George Shelvocke, reached 61°30'S during the austral summer of 1719–20. Shelvocke's book of his journey included an account of the shooting of an albatross. This was read by William Wordsworth who in turn suggested to his friend Samuel Taylor Coleridge that he use the incident in the epic poem he was then writing. Coleridge substituted a crossbow for the shotgun used by Shelvocke's man and used the killing as the central theme of *The Rime of the Ancient Mariner*. Both poles, therefore, can claim some credit for the work.

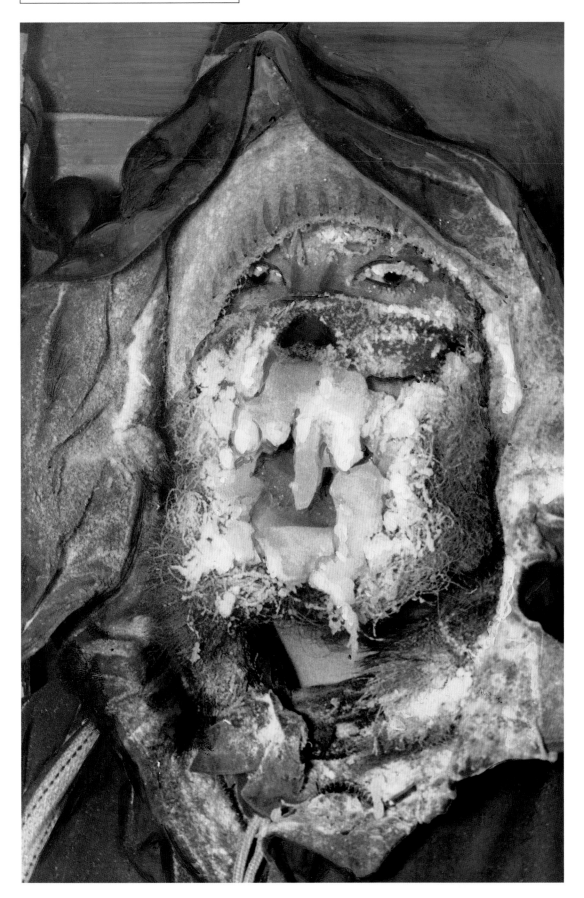

left
The popular image of polar exploration is exemplified by this photo of Lt Angus Erskine, a member of the British North Greenland Expedition which surveyed the northern island from 1952 to 1954. Lt Erskine was caught in a blizzard.

There is little doubt that Amundsen was the greatest of all polar explorers: first man to the South Pole; probably among the first to see the North Pole; first through the NW Passage; second west-east transit of the NE Passage; first overwinter in Antarctica. Yet for all his achievements he remains an enigmatic man, to whom the Norwegians never took to as they did to Nansen. Amundsen became increasingly embittered as he grew older, feeling that the fame he was due was being unjustly withheld. He also did himself harm with an act which started out surprising everyone for its kindness. During the Maud expedition Amundsen rescued two young Chukchi girls from extreme poverty. Kakonita was motherless, dirty and lice-infested, while Camilla was of mixed race and consequently unwanted by her tribe. Amundsen took them to Oslo as foster children, offering them to be a home, security and an education. But eventually Amundsen grew tired of the girls and packed them off to Seattle for a return to Chukchi and an uncertain future. In fact the two settled in America and lived contented lives there, but that was no thanks to Amundsen.

The crew of *Gjøa* after the ship had reached Nome in Alaska. Amundsen is to the left.

Rae obtained from the Inuit relics which were clearly from the expedition. These, and the tale of lingering death and cannibalism, he brought to Britain. The reaction of officialdom and the press was outrage. The Times castigated Rae for believing the word of Inuit as they 'like all savages are liars'. Charles Dickens published articles in which he developed this theme and also insisted that no Englishman could possibly have stooped so low as even to contemplate cannibalism. Far more likely was that the Inuit had murdered Franklin's men, perhaps even eating them as well, and were now trying to shift the blame on to the innocent victims. Rae was condemned for having been duped. Despite his efforts in the Arctic, which included a very real claim to having discovered the southern North-West Passage (the route eventually followed by Amundsen), Rae never received the knighthood he rightly thought was his due.

Despite the controversy over Rae's discoveries, the Admiralty still refused to send another expedition, and Lady Jane, keener than ever to discover the truth, financed another, Francis McClintock sailing in 1857. After overwintering twice, McClintock's men finally found evidence suggesting Rae's tale was correct. All along the western shore of King William Island

In the Arctic, explorers had to face the challenges of hostile terrain and climate. There was also the possibility of attack by polar bears, which are not just the world's largest but also the only truly carnivorous bears. The early explorers probably took a less relaxed attitude to that of these observers of a female and two cubs swimming off Greenland's north-eastern coast.

THE NORTH-WEST PASSAGE

The quest for a North-West Passage, a navigable route westwards along the northern coast of the Americas to Asia, became something of a Holy Grail to early European explorers. After its early failures, Britain realised that the search for the Passage was futile and turned its attention to the land, ousting the French and setting up the Hudson's Bay Company to exploit the fur-bearing animals of the Arctic rim. A Company man, Samuel Hearne, followed the Coppermine River and Alexander Mackenzie went down the Mackenzie River and later became the first European to view the Pacific Ocean from the North American coast.

In the wake of the Napoleonic Wars, the quest for a North-West Passage was resurrected as a means of occupying Britain's large and temporarily redundant navy. Naval officers were sent on both land and sea journeys, filling in the gaps in the mapping of the northern coast of Canada. John Ross rediscovered Baffin Bay. William Edward Parry won a prize for becoming the first man to reach 110°W, overwintering successfully on Melville Island. On land John Franklin retraced Hearne's journey down the Coppermine. On later journeys Parry found the Fury and Hecla Strait, named for his ships, while Franklin retraced Mackenzie's journey, then turned west to reach Herschel Island. Here Franklin was stopped by bad weather: he was less than 250 kms (about 155 miles) from the most easterly point reached, Frederick Beechey heading east from the Pacific. Had Franklin met Beechey later history might have been changed.

Following the string of failures to find the Passage, or much else of great interest, the British public became apathetic about further attempts and naval expeditions ceased. Exploration did not. Hudson's Bay Company men continued to carry out valuable work. One was John Rae who proved that the Boothia Peninsula was part of the mainland, not an island as had been thought. In 1828 John Ross was engaged by Felix Booth, bottler of the famous gin (and for whom Boothia Peninsula is named), to have one more try to discover the Passage. Ross failed, but his young nephew, James Clark Ross, who accompanied him, reached the North Magnetic Pole.

Back in Britain the Admiralty, concerned that the relative success of private expeditions was making its own efforts look ridiculous, decided to try one more time. Looking around for a likely commander they discovered that all their Arctic men were either retired or disinclined. Only one man was willing, his willingness due in large part to the enthusiasm of his young wife Jane who wished to see her husband given the credit he was due for a long and distinguished career. Under Jane's relentless pressure the navy eventually gave in and appointed John Franklin to the command.

John Franklin's is one of the most famous names in Arctic exploration, his entry into history coinciding with the new art of photography. In 1845 Franklin took the *Terror* and *Erebus* west. They were spotted by a whaler in Baffin Bay but after that neither ship, nor Franklin or any of his 128 men, were ever seen alive again.

left
This early daguerreotype shows John Franklin at the time the expedition sailed. It shows an old and overweight man (he was almost 60) – not really the expected image of a man suited for command of an Arctic expedition lasting several years.

As expeditions had frequently gone for years without any news arriving back in Britain there was no concern at first. Then, gradually, it began to dawn on the authorities that Franklin was not coming back. By 1848 rescue expeditions were being sent out, the number of these growing as the years passed. Spurred on by the formidable Lady Franklin, and the press who sided with her, the Admiralty sent ship after ship. Lady Jane also appealed to the Americans, several of the more famous US Arctic explorers, particularly Charles Francis Hall, gaining valuable experience on Franklin search parties. The search also mapped most of the islands of Arctic Canada as the searching ships looked, in vain, for any trace of the missing expedition. In 1850 Robert McClure sailed east from the Bering Strait and discovered the northern passage, though he completed the crossing by sledge when his ships were iced in. Despite this, back in Britain McClure received a knighthood and, after much complaining, the reward for discovering the passage, a reward he declined to share either with his crew or his rescuers, a decision which appalled everyone except himself.

While McClure was searching in the east, the first trace of Franklin was found in the west where, on Beechey Island, three graves and a cairn of food were found. More than a century after they were buried the men who occupied the graves were exhumed and examined by a Canadian team. The men, their bodies perfectly preserved in the deep freeze of the permafrost, were shown to have died of natural causes but to have had high levels of lead in their systems which would have exacerbated any illness. It is conjectured that the expedition, one of the first

to use tinned food, had been poisoned by the lead of the solder which sealed the cans. Recently it has been suggested that the contents of the tins – poor-quality food prepared in distinctly unhygienic conditions – may have been contaminated, food poisoning further reducing the men's ability to overcome the rigours of the Arctic winter. But three graves and a pile of food tins did not solve the mystery of what had happened to Franklin. The Admiralty had by now lost half-a-dozen ships and were becoming weary of the effort. Franklin had been gone six years and no one except Lady Franklin thought he was alive. Quietly they shelved plans for further rescue attempts, though Lady Jane continued to finance her own search.

In 1853 John Rae, the Hudson's Bay Company man, led a land expedition in search of Franklin, finding Inuit who told him of a large group of white men who had been seen heading south along King William Island's western shore. The men had been exhausted and reduced to cannibalism by extreme hunger. None had survived.

left
Dr John Rae in 1862. After the savagery of the attacks on him by British society and the press, Rae continued to explore in northern Canada making several important journeys. He died in London in 1893, aged 79. His wife took his body to the Orkneys where he had spent his childhood. He is buried behind St Magnus Cathedral in Kirkwall.

left
Amundsen's ship *Gjøa*, now preserved in Oslo outside the museum which has been constructed over Fram. The ship is surprisingly small considering the epic nature of the journey through the North-West Passage.

above
Sir Francis McClintock. Despite confirming Rae's story about the fate of Franklin, McClintock did rather better out of the tragedy. He was knighted, promoted to Admiral, made a freeman of the city of London, given several honorary degrees, a gold medal by the Royal Geographical Society and a fat reward. He is also mentioned below Franklin's bust in Westminster Abbey.

The 5th Thule - Ekspedision 1921-24
The northwest passage -
Knud Rasmussen

were the remains of Franklin's expedition, these including skeletons and ship's boats and, in a cairn, a note that said that Franklin had died in 1847 and that the two ships had been abandoned in the ice off the island. The surviving members of the expedition had headed south towards the Great Fish River which no doubt they hoped would lead them to a Hudson's Bay Company fort. King William Island is a desolate, unforgiving place. With food running low the exhausted men died along the way, the last of them dying after resorting to cannibalism. As a tale of horror and despair, long drawn out and hopeless, the Franklin expedition has few equals, even if the real story will never be known.

The British gave up any thoughts of completing the passage after Franklin. The country had been mapped; if it could be sailed at all the passage was not a commercially viable waterway. And so it was forgotten for half a century, until the 31-year-old Norwegian Roald Amundsen took up the challenge. Reasoning, correctly, that much of the problem with the British attempts had been the use of ships that were too big, he headed west in a small herring boat called *Gjøa* (pronounced you-ah) with a crew of seven. The Norwegians sailed through Lancaster Sound, then south through Peel Strait and around King William Island to winter in what is now Gjøahaven. After two winters there *Gjøa* sailed west to Herschel Island from where Amundsen sledged south to Eagle City to announce the news that he had successfully sailed the North-West Passage. Technically, of course, Amundsen was premature, *Gjøa* not actually completing the voyage until the following year when it rounded Point Barrow and sailed through the Bering Strait.

above
The first commercial transit of the North-West Passage. Escorted by the Canadian icebreaker *John A McDonald*, the 155,000-ton US tanker *Manhattan* made the transit in 1969 using the northern route. As the ice shrinks northward, a shrinkage which is consistent with, but does not prove, global

warming, the possibility that the medieval dream of a commercial northern route from the Atlantic to the Pacific draws ever closer.

above top
In 1923–24 as part of the Fifth Thule Expedition (a series of journeys aimed at exploring Inuit culture as well as filling in final gaps in the Arctic maps)

the Dane, Knud Rasmussen followed the Passage by land with dog sledges over the ice. This photo shows the returning sun after winter on the ice. Rasmussen's journey was repeated, solo, by the Japanese Naomi Uemura in 1974–76 and then in 1991–93 by a young Spaniard, Ramón Hernando de Larramendi.

left
Cape Dezhnev, the
easternmost point of
Asia. On top of the rise
is a lighthouse/memorial
to Semen Dezhnev. The
other buildings are said
to be research
accommodation, but
with Alaska just across
the Straits it is possible
they were also used for
more clandestine
operations.

THE NORTH-EAST PASSAGE

In the mid-16th century the discovery of a narwhal tusk on the shores of the Kara Sea, off Russia's northern coast, sparked interest in a north-eastern route to the Orient. As the toothed whale was unknown, the object was clearly a unicorn horn, and it was 'known' that 'Unycorns are bredde in the landes of Cathaye, Chynayne and other Oriental Regions'. The British headed that way, as did the Dutchman Willem Barents, who was forced to overwinter on Novaya Zemlya where he and many of his crew died of scurvy. These attempts were stopped by the ice of the Kara Sea, and for a century the area was left to the native Arctic dwellers.

Then, in need of wealth to breathe life into the failing Russian economy, Ivan the Terrible allowed the cossack (from the Chinese word for a man with no king, and later meaning a frontiersman) Ermak to annex Siberia, giving Russia access to its apparently limitless wealth of animal furs. The Russians quickly marched across the vastness of Siberia reaching the Kolyma River by 1642. Then in 1648, in response to rumours of unimaginable riches in sable furs, an expedition was sent out under the protection of the cossack Semen Ivanovich Dezhnev. Encountering favourable ice conditions, Dezhnev rounded what is now called Cape Dezhnev, the Chukchi Peninsula's north-eastern tip, and sighted the Diomede islands. The expedition had passed through the strait that separates Russia and north America, but as the record

left
Vitus Bering. Recently a Danish–Russian expedition located the graves of the men, exhuming Bering's skeleton and recreating his head from the skull. It was discovered that the standard portrait of Bering was not of him at all, but most likely a relative of his mother.

of the journey was lost for over a century, this piece of water is now called the Bering Strait after a later explorer.

Vitus Bering was a 44-year-old Dane entrusted by Peter the Great to explore east of Chukchi to see if Russia was joined to America. History has been kind to Bering – James Cook, unaware of Dezhnev's journey, named the Strait for him despite Bering never actually having sailed through it. Bering reached St Lawrence Island, but he did not see Alaska and observed only that the local Chukchi coast turned east, not west, before turning south for home. Moscow was not impressed, but strangely was persuaded to give Bering command of a second expedition, on which Europeans landed on Alaska for the first time. Bering and many other members of his crew died of scurvy on one of the Commander Islands, one now called Bering Island in his honour.

Bering's second expedition was a part of what became known as the Great Northern Expedition, an enterprise which surveyed the entire north coast of Russia from the White Sea to Chukchi, and the east coast as far as Japan. This was a monumental exercise, and was completed within a decade. Following the success of the Great Northern Expedition the idea of a North-East Passage was revived. Yet, strangely, it was not a Russian who completed the first transit, but a Swede, Adolf Erik Nordenskiöld, born in Finland of Swedish parents. Nordenskiöld was already an experienced Arctic traveller when in 1878 he acquired the *Vega*, a 300-ton, three-masted whaler with a steam engine. With a crew totalling 30 he sailed from Karlskrona in southern Sweden reaching the Kara Sea in early August. It was ice-free,

right
Nordenskiöld's ship, the *Vega*, arrived in Stockholm on 24 April 1880 (now known as Vega Day in Sweden) after his epic voyage through the North-East Passage and back to Sweden. Here the ship is anchored below the Royal Palace where King Oscar II gave a reception and dinner for captain and crew.

above
The only photo of Nordenskiöld taken on board the *Vega*.

allowing Nordenskiöld to continue to Cape Chelyuskin where 'the landscape was the dullest and most desolate I have seen in the high north'. By late September, Nordenskiöld estimated he was two days' sailing from Cape Dezhnev, but then ice stopped the ship.

The winter was spent comfortably, the *Vega* being freed from the ice in July 1879. Two days later Nordenskiöld passed Cape Dezhnev and reached the Bering Strait. The completion of the North-East Passage had been a masterpiece of good organisation and seamanship, and is one of the greatest of all polar voyages. But for Nordenskiöld it was merely an hors d'oeuvre, the *Vega* sailing on to Japan, then around China to the Indian Ocean and on to the Suez Canal. She sailed across the Mediterranean, then around Portugal to the English Channel and the North Sea, finally reaching Sweden in April 1880.

left and above
The third transit, and second west–east transit, was made by Roald Amundsen in the *Maud* in 1918–20, an expedition during which two men died as they attempted to reach civilisation after leaving the ship. The reasons why the pair left seem straightforward, but are still debated, adding another controversy to Amundsen's story. Following the expedition, *Maud* was sold to the Hudson's Bay Company. Renamed *Baymaud* she was used as an Arctic supply vessel until she sank in Cambridge Bay. There, her rotting spars can still be seen.

below left
The *Chelyuskin* incident. In the foreground, survivors from the ship erect the camp in which they lived for two months before being rescued by air. In the background the ship's angle suggests that the shot was taken not long before she sank.

After the disastrous defeat in the Russo–Japanese War of 1904–05, the Russian government realised the advantages of a Northern Sea Route, as they called the North-East Passage, and built two ice breakers to explore its possibilities. In these, an expedition under the command of Boris Andreyevich Vilkitskiy, starting from Vladivostok in 1914, completed the second transit of the passage, and the first east–west transit, by reaching Archangel in 1915.

In July 1932 the sealer *Aleksandr Sibiryakov* completed the first transit (going west–east) in a single season, this encouraging the Soviet authorities to send a fleet of 11 ships eastwards in 1933. One was the 4,000 ton *Chelyuskin*, not an ice-breaker, but sufficiently large to nose through significant ice. Entering a narrow lead off Chukchi, the *Chelyuskin* became ice-bound, drifting into Bering Strait, then north-west towards Wrangel Island. After wintering in the ice, on 13 February 1934 the ship was crushed and sank. The 104 survivors set up a camp on the ice from which they were rescued by planes which landed on a runway carved from the sea ice. Following the loss of the *Chelyuskin* there were further transits of the passage in the 1930s, but it has never become a regular route either for Soviet/Russian or other shipping. The passage has also had commercial tourist transits, though these too have been limited in number. Even if global warming should reduce the ice cover north of Siberia, it is likely that Russian nervousness about foreign vessels venturing near its northern shore will mean that transits will never become frequent.

above
Stalin was so delighted by the show of Soviet abilities during the rescue of the *Chelyuskin* survivors that the seven pilots involved were the first to receive the award of Hero of the Soviet Union. Anatoli Lyapidevski, who made the first flight, was the first recipient. Here Stalin is presented with a memento of the rescue.

CANADA

Although the search for the North-West Passage had mapped the coastline of north America and discovered many of Canada's Arctic islands, there was still a vast uncharted area north of the transit line.

In 1902 Otto Sverdrup, captain of the *Fram* on Nansen's expedition, led his own expedition, also in *Fram*, exploring Ellesmere Island's west coast and discovering Axel Heiberg and the Ringnes Islands. Norway's early claim for sovereignty over the islands awakened Canada's latent interest and led to a series of national expeditions to the far north. The early trips were under the command of the Quebecois Joseph-Elzéar Bernier, but in 1913 the Canadian government gave command of an expedition to Vilhjalmur Stefansson, Canadian-born, but of Icelandic parents.

Stefansson's ship was the *Karluk*, its journey becoming an Arctic contemporary of Shackleton's *Endurance*. The ship followed the same pattern – beset in the ice and sinking, the crew facing a difficult journey to land. But there was to be no joyful ending, the *Karluk* crew's retreat being a harrowing tale of death and misery. Nor was their journey behind the guiding light of a great leader, the tale – largely ignored for decades, but recently revived – adding another chapter to the story of a controversial explorer.

The *Karluk* was captained by Bob Bartlett, then considered by many the finest ice captain on the planet. Bartlett had serious reservations about the ship and also about the lack of organisation of the expedition, but nevertheless took *Karluk* northwards in June 1913, heading for Herschel Island, the expedition's winter base. But *Karluk*'s lack of speed meant that when winter came the ship was some way off Herschel and trapped in unrelenting ice. At this point Stefansson announced that he was heading for the shore to hunt caribou and would be gone 10 days. He did not return, but reached Herschel Island from where he sent a message to Ottawa that the ship was entombed in ice and might, or might not,

sink. Those on board, he said, would probably survive. Stefansson then headed north to find a continent he was sure lay in the Arctic Ocean.

The *Karluk* and its 25 passengers and crew drifted west to the Bering Strait, then on towards Siberia. On 10 January 1914 the ice finally ruptured the hull. Bartlett now took his crew south towards Wrangel. Four men disappeared on the march, their remains being found years later on the desolate Herald Island. The rest reached Wrangel, but the security the island offered was illusory – Wrangel was uninhabited and animals for food were sparse. Taking one companion, Bartlett therefore crossed the thinning ice sheet to Siberia where he found a village. After resting and eating, Bartlett travelled 650 km (400 miles) to the shore of the Bering Strait and found a ship bound for Alaska.

On Wrangel the situation was now desperate: one frostbitten man needed amputations to stop gangrene, these being carried out by penknife and hacksaw blade. Another man died of a gunshot wound to the head: whether murder or suicide has never been established. Two more died of

starvation, cold and exhaustion. Those remaining were finally rescued by a ship alerted by Bartlett. While war raged in Europe nothing was heard of Stefansson and it was assumed that he, too, had died. Then in 1918, after five years out of contact, he returned. He had found the last three islands of Canada's Arctic archipelago but had not discovered the continent he craved. Despite his abandonment of his expedition and the hideous outcome for those left on the *Karluk*, Stefansson's remarkable survival meant he died a hero while the real hero, Bob Bartlett, was for many years largely ignored.

GREENLAND

In the early 18th century, Denmark sent Hans Egede, a young pastor, to Greenland to look for surviving remnants of the Viking settlers. Egede found no trace, but the visit cemented the Danish claim to the country, one which they have maintained, though Greenland now has home rule.

Greenland's southern coast had been explored by whalers, but the ice-blocked seas of the north and the interior of the country were still unknown. Nordenskiöld, discoverer of the North-East Passage, was one of the first to head inland, certain that the vast inland ice cap was merely a coastal ring hiding a forested centre. His team penetrated about 200 km (125 miles) in 1883 but saw no trace of this assumed forest.

The next to try, in 1886, was Robert Peary, an ambitious American whose name was soon to become synonymous with attempts to reach the North Pole. Peary did not get as far as Nordenskiöld did, but believed that his attempt gave him proprietorial rights over the inland ice and was furious when a young Norwegian, Fridtjof Nansen, crossed Greenland, proving that the interior was an enormous ice cap.

Nansen, who was later to become a distinguished diplomat and winner of the Nobel Peace Prize, started from the east side of Greenland, the opposite side from which Nordenskiöld and Peary had tried. He later claimed that as the east side was largely uninhabited and therefore offered little hope of retreat, this ensured that his team would press on at all costs — death or the west coast, as he put it. More likely is the fact that the west coast had a number of established settlements, which gave him more options in

above

Armed with the single stick then used for cross-country skiing (double sticks not becoming popular until a few years later) the young Fridtjof Nansen was the very image of a Viking. He was popular with ladies (Nansen was having an affair with Scott's wife as her husband was dying in Antarctica), but less so with his team-mates who found him arrogant and overbearing.

terms of route: had Nordenskiöld or Peary actually reached the east coast, they would have had to turn around and return, something which Nansen was able to avoid. Nansen's team of five (six with himself) included Otto Sverdrup, and a man who later confessed he had only agreed to go because he was drunk at the time. On the ice cap they manhauled sledges, using primitive sails to help with the work. The west coast (close to Nuuk, Greenland's capital) was reached, after 40 days on the ice.

Peary responded to Nansen's journey by accusing the Norwegian of cheating, and then making his own crossing, west to east, in the unexplored far north of the country. One member of Peary's small team was Dr Frederick Cook, a man who was later to become Peary's bitter rival in the race for the North Pole. Using dog teams, and sending part of the team back early in the

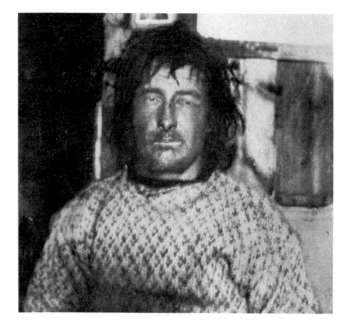 

above and right
The photographs of Mikkelsen (left) and Iversen (right) after their ordeal show a pair of wild-eyed men driven half to madness by enforced isolation and continuous suffering. Their story is perhaps the greatest tale of polar survival.

trek to maximise the supplies for those continuing – a technique the British later employed in the Antarctic – Peary made a remarkable crossing of Greenland. Unfortunately his mis-observation of the form of the west coast (believing he saw a waterway, the Peary Channel) was later to prove fatal to a Danish expedition. Peary made several more trips to north-west Greenland, adding to the understanding of the area's geography, but increasingly his lust for fame drew him into attempts to reach the Pole, leaving the Danes to fill in the last blank sections of Greenland's coastal map.

The first Danish expedition, seduced by Peary's insistence that a waterway split the northern island, ended in disaster, three men dying as they attempted to retreat from mapping the true shape of north-east Greenland. A second expedition was sent, a body from the first trip being buried at the expense of one man sustaining frostbitten toes which had to be amputated using only a bottle of whisky as anaesthetic. Then two men, Ejnar Mikkelsen and Iver Iversen, went north alone to find the other bodies. What they did not know was that during their absence the expedition ship, the *Alabama*, sank. Mikkelsen and Iversen failed to find the bodies of their countrymen, but did find a note detailing the geography of the north-east and the fact that the Peary Channel did not exist. The two men then started south, soon experiencing the same appalling conditions of wet snow that had slowed, then killed the previous team. On the verge of starvation the pair eventually reached their start point, only to discover the ship sunk and their team mates gone. Forced to overwinter, the two survived by hunting but the hoped-for rescue failed to materialise the next summer and they were forced to overwinter again. Only the following summer were they rescued.

Today, in keeping with its status as the largest northern-hemisphere wilderness, Greenland attracts many expeditions each year, the crossing of its ice cap having become a virtual rite of passage for young explorers. Yet despite the fact that crossings of the inland ice have become run of the mill, the sheer size of the island has allowed modern explorers scope for astonishing feats. In 1978 the Japanese Naomi Uemura used a dog sledge to traverse the ice cap along its 'long axis', the first such traverse, achieved solo and after first making a solo journey to the North Pole. Then in 1996 two Norwegians, Rune Gjeldnes

above
On the Greenland ice cap during the epic south–north traverse of Rune Gjeldnes and Torry Larsen. The beautiful weather belies the epic qualities of the trip.

below
The Pomores, natives of Russia's north-western Arctic shore, were famous for their sea voyages. It is conjectured that they may have made early journeys to Russia's Arctic islands, and also to Svalbard. This Russian cross on Kvitøya shows that Russians certainly visited Svalbard, though the date of such journeys is still debated.

and Torry Larsen, parachuted on to the southern inland ice on 19 March, determined to make the first complete north–south traverse of Greenland. Abseiling down the ice front, they used kayaks in an attempt to paddle to, and around, Kapp Farvel (Cape Farewell), Greenland's southernmost point. This attempt was defeated by weather which made the crossing dangerous, though the two did come within sight of the cape. Having paddled back to the mainland they regained the ice cap and using sails to aid the towing of 175-kg sleds they skied north reaching Cape Morris Jesup where they were collected by air. Their trek of 2,930 km (1,830 miles) was the longest unsupported ski journey at that time, but has lately been bettered by others in Antarctica.

RUSSIA

In 1745 a silk map was sewn for the Czar showing the results of the Great Northern War. It delineated the northern coast of mainland Russia but showed only one archipelago, Novaya Zemlya, of the four that lie off Russia's Arctic coast. A few years later a second island group, the New Siberian Islands, was discovered after a hunter noticed a group of reindeer walking towards him from off the sea ice. Reasoning the animals must be coming from land he followed their tracks north, discovering an island on which he found clear signs that other hunters had preceded him, but remained silent so that they could exploit the islands in peace.

The most northerly island group, Franz Josef Land, was found in 1873 by an Austro–Hungarian expedition. This expedition, aboard the *Tegetthof*, was attempting, in the face of all known facts, to sail north over the Pole to China. Becoming trapped in the ice the crew were forced to overwinter, carried north by the drifting ice. One day, when fog which had shrouded them for days lifted, the men were amazed to see land which they named for their Emperor. When the hoped-for release of the ship did not materialise the men abandoned her and marched south across the pack ice. After many weeks of arduous travel they resighted the ship, realising that days of hard effort had been wiped out by the drift of the

ice. Desperate, but realising that to regain the ship was futile, they set out again, this time reaching Novaya Zemlya where, on the brink of starvation, they were rescued by a Russian ship.

The final archipelago, Severnaya Zemlya, was not found until the early years of the 20th century, with the expeditions of Vilkitskiy which culminated in the first east–west transit of the North-East Passage. Vilkitskiy used two ice-breakers, each modelled on the world's first ice-breaker, the *Ermak*. Though *Ermak* was Russian in concept and ownership, the ship was actually built in Newcastle-upon-Tyne, England in 1898. *Ermak* was the brainchild of Vice-Admiral Markov of the Russian navy and was used in an attempt to reach the North Pole in 1899, which failed at 81°28′N. That attempt, and the later enthusiasm for transits of the North-East Passage, led to an expedition which has only recently received the interest it deserves.

The *Saint Anna* left Murmansk in September 1914, far too late in the year for an attempt on the passage, the decision indicating the lack of experience of the ship's captain, Georgi Brusilov. Soon the ship was ice-bound, and after two winters, had drifted towards the northern tip of Franz Josef Land. At that point relations between Brusilov and his deputy Valerian Albanov broke down, and Albanov decided to leave the ship and walk south. Together with 13 men who feared the ship was doomed, Albanov set out on the 120 km (74 miles) walk to Franz Josef. After 11 days of exhausting effort the men had walked just 5 km (3 miles) south, but drifted 22 km (13 miles) north: three men then abandoned the attempt and returned to the ship. The rest continued, shooting seals for food and fuel (heating water by burning blubber) and using kayaks when they reached occasional stretches of open water. After 10 weeks they reached Franz Josef. By now, men were dying of exhaustion, but Albanov kept them marching, finding a note left by Frederick Jackson that finally fixed his position. The survivors now split into groups. Some used kayaks while others skied, Albanov and another man being split off from their group of kayakers and almost killed by a violent storm. Eventually Albanov and his companion Konrad reached Cape Flora where they found another Russian expedition. Of their comrades nothing was ever seen again. The *Saint Anna* and the remaining crew also disappeared without trace.

TO THE POLE

The first genuine attempt on the Pole was made in 1773 by Englishman Constantine Phipps whose crew included a 14-year-old midshipman called Horatio Nelson who narrowly avoided being killed by a polar bear. Phipps was followed by Parry, hero of the North-West Passage. Parry's attempt to manhaul sledges on which rested the ship's boats (in case open water was found) was doomed by the

THE WALLSEND SLIPWAY
AND
ENGINEERING CO LTD
ENGINES Nº 491
1899.
NEWCASTLE ON TYNE.

sheer effort required: occasionally his team made only 250 m (820 ft) of headway in an hour of hard pulling. In 1872, Parry reached 82°45'N, a record at the time.

The next attempts were American. Elisha Kent Kane headed north in 1855, his surgeon on that trip, Isaac Hayes, trying again in 1860. But these were primarily Franklin search expeditions, the first genuine American trip being in 1871 when Charles Francis Hall sailed the *Polaris* north between Ellesmere Island and Greenland. The attempt ended in tragedy, Hall dying and being buried on Greenland's shore, and the expedition breaking up in confusion. Some team members were left on an ice floe when the ship was unexpectedly driven away by a gale, though both these men and those on the ship survived.

Following Hall's attempt the British tried once more, George Nares sailing two ships to Ellesmere's northern shore, one of the most remarkable feats of seamanship in polar history. From the winter camp Lieutenant Albert Markham took a sledge party north, establishing a new northing record of 83°20'26"N on 12 May 1876. Despite the brilliance of Nares' seamanship, the new record and the considerable exploration undertaken, the expedition almost ended in disaster, 80 per cent of the men contracting scurvy. Years before, John Rae had realised that fresh meat, fish and vegetables were effective anti-scorbutants, and it was well known that lime juice aged badly and so became less effective with time. But a committee set up to investigate the shortcomings of the Nares trip concluded that nothing could have been

below left
During the attempt to resupply Greely's expedition, the *Proteus* was trapped in the ice and sank. The ship had been under the command of Ernest Garlington, an odd choice as he was a cavalry officer, promoted when many of the officers on his unit, the 7th Cavalry, were killed with Custer at the Little Big Horn. Garlington later won the Congressional Medal of Honor for his part in the infamous attack on the Indians at Wounded Knee.

below
Suspicion over Hall's death existed from the day it was reported, but was confirmed by an exhumation and autopsy carried out in 1968, which showed that Hall had died of arsenic poisoning. Whether this was self-administered during a bout of prolonged ill-health, or whether it was murder, cannot now be established. Many favour the latter, but the name and motive of any guilty party remains elusive.

right
Greely's tent,
photographed by the
expedition's rescuers.
Evidence of cannibalism
found at the camp was
hushed up in the official
enquiry which tactfully
decided that any flesh
which had been
removed from dead
bodies had been taken
'with a view no doubt to
use as shrimp bait'.

improved, either on the matter of anti-scorbutants or equipment. One of the committee was a cousin of Albert Markham: Clements Markham was later instrumental in appointing Robert Falcon Scott to lead the expeditions to Antarctica.

The Americans were back in 1881, Adolphus Washington Greely taking the *Proteus* north to Nares, winter camp and establishing a base – Fort Conger – there. The *Proteus* then sailed south again. Greely's trip had a dual purpose: he intended to reach the Pole but was also carrying out scientific studies. The first objective failed, though James Lockwood led a team which passed Markham's record by 6.5 km (4 miles).

The second objective was achieved, Ellesmere Island being explored, but things then began to go wrong. The expected relief ship failed to appear and, with food running low and another winter approaching, Greely decided to abandon Fort Conger, taking his expedition south to Cape Sabine where the relief ship was supposed to have dropped supplies if it could not reach Fort Conger. Reaching the Cape, Greely found no supplies – it was going to be a long, hungry winter. A relief expedition had been sent, the *Proteus* again, but had become entombed in ice and sank. Though the crew survived, back in the US the Secretary of War, Robert Lincoln, son of Abraham, vetoed a further attempt to go north. Greely had been abandoned.

On Pym Island near Cape Sabine, Greely's men built a rough hut of stone around an upturned boat. The area was devoid of animals and as winter approached the men were forced on to starvation rations. Soup was made by boiling rope and boot soles, then the buffalo hide sleeping bags which were the men's only protection against the cold. One man caught stealing food was court-martialled, sentenced to death and shot. The expedition doctor died the same day, probably a suicide by self-administered drugs. By spring the few men left alive were eating candles, what was left of old leather strips, seaweed and anything else they could find. But now, back in Washington the consciences of the nation's governors were finally pricked and a rescue was organised. It found just seven of 25 men alive. One of the rescued men died soon after: the frostbite of his hands and feet was so bad that bones stuck out from the rotting flesh and even amputation could not save him.

Two years before Greely set out, another American expedition had headed north. Led by George

Wilson not only declined his invitation to join the party, but took Scott's side when he denied Shackleton use of the *Discovery* base. Worse, Wilson also sided with Scott's view that Shackleton should not go anywhere near the Ross Sea. Appalled by this, Shackleton nevertheless agreed to stay east of 170°W.

Like Scott, Shackleton visited Nansen. Scott had half-heartedly agreed to take dogs and skis after his visit, but Shackleton amazed Nansen by announcing that he would not use skis, preferring to walk, and would take ponies rather than dogs. Exactly why is disputed, but it is difficult not to see the influence of Frederick Jackson, the Englishman who had met Nansen in Franz Josef Land. Jackson had compared dogs and ponies on his expedition: the dogs had come out best every time, but mystifyingly Jackson had claimed the opposite, even telling Nansen as much (and being advised by Nansen to think again). The fact that Shackleton was planning to take a vegetarian animal to the only continent on earth where there was virtually no vegetation seems to have been subsumed by the idea that ponies represented food on the hoof, food in very large packets, food without the killing problems of dogs that upset the squeamish.

When *Nimrod* reached Antarctica, ice conditions and lack of time forced Shackleton to break his promise to Scott, though he did build a new hut at Cape Royds, 35 kms (21 miles) further from the Pole. After overwintering, Shackleton decided on two objectives: he would lead a team of four south while Edgworth David would lead a three-man team in an attempt to reach the South Magnetic Pole. Shackleton passed Scott's record southing, then forged a route up the Beardmore Glacier on to the polar plateau. Despite the misgivings of his team, all of whom were suffering exhaustion, hunger and hypothermia, Shackleton insisted on pushing on when it became clear they did not have the supplies to reach the pole. Finally, having reached 88°23'S and so being less than 160 kms (100 miles) from the pole – Shackleton's second target – the men turned around.

The return journey was a nightmare, the four on the edge of starvation for almost the whole 1,170 kms (727 miles). Several times they ran out of food altogether and only luck with the weather allowed them to reach the

right
Left to right: Adams, Wild and Shackleton at their
furthest south. Realising the pole was not attainable,
Shackleton forced the men on until he had reached a
point less than 160 kms (100 miles) from it. Back in
Britain some argued that the team's final position could
not have been as far south as he claimed – the team had
not taken the theodolite on their last dash to the 160 kms
(100 miles) barrier – but Roald Amundsen noted that if
Shackleton had travelled the same distance from the Bay
of Whales, he would probably have made it all the way. It
was shrewd observation.

next supply dump: bad weather would inevitably have meant death. All collapsed at some point, Eric
Marshall, the team doctor, taking the lead at one stage when Shackleton fell ill. Finally arriving at the
hut they found that everyone, and the *Nimrod*, had gone, but unbelievably the ship returned at just the
right moment.

With the return of the ship, Shackleton found that the magnetic Pole team (David, Mawson and
Mackay) had triumphed, a major success which went some way to easing his disappointment at failing
to reach the Pole. Back in Britain he was given a hero's welcome and a knighthood.

Amundsen had actually intended to head for the North Pole, but news that Cook and/or Peary had
reached it made him turn south. Aware that the British would cry foul and that Nansen, who had loaned
him *Fram*, would be displeased as he wished to use *Fram* the following year for his own attempt to reach
the South Pole, Amundsen kept his intentions secret for as long as he could. Reaching the Ross Sea he
set up a base at the Bay of Whales, then used what was left of the autumn to set up bases to 82°S.
When he had arrived in Antarctica, Amundsen had been 480 kms (298 miles) behind Scott. He was now,
effectively, 240 kms (149 miles) ahead.

Nervous of the motorised sledges he knew Scott had, Amundsen made the mistake of setting off too
early for the pole in the austral spring of 1911 and was forced to retreat by temperatures which fell to
-57°C. The retreat was a shambles, the expedition being saved by Hjalmar Johansen – Nansen's
companion on his northern dash from *Fram*. Johansen was furious with Amundsen who, fearing a
breakdown of his leadership, sacked Johansen from the pole team. It was a bitter blow to Johansen,
who already thought himself rejected by Nansen, and contributed to Johansen's suicide. That was a sad

above top
The *Endurance* frozen in
at 76°35'S. As well as his
famous series of black
and white prints Frank
Hurley, the expedition's
photographer, took a
small number of 'Paget'
plates, an early form of
colour photography which
used dyed screens to
produce a basic colour
image. The cost and the
fact that enlargements
showed the screen

pattern meant the
technique never caught
on. It is difficult to
produce a colour image
from Hurley's original
plates, but they do offer a
fascinating view of
Shackleton's expedition.

above

Another of Hurley's
Paget plates. This one
shows Ernest Shackleton
watching a lead form in
the Weddell Sea.

This forced Ernest Shackleton, still wanting to leave his mark on Antarctica, to seek private funds for his proposed traverse of the continent from the Weddell to the Ross seas. His ship, *Endurance*, left Britain on 1 August 1914. On 4 August Britain declared war on Germany. Shackleton offered his services to the war effort, but was told to continue. Today the expedition is seen as triumphant, but it is worth remembering that at the time there were many who thought that brave, fit men should have been heading towards, not away from, the conflict.

The story of the *Endurance* is now so well known it does not require a long retelling. Shackleton's attempt to reach the coast of the Weddell Sea was thwarted by the ice which first held, then sank his ship. Forced to abandon their attempted traverse, the team drifted north on the sea-ice, then used the ship's boats to reach the hostile, uninhabited Elephant Island. From there Shackleton and five others made what is still considered to be the most remarkable sea journey of all time, taking an open boat across the raging Southern Ocean to reach South Georgia. Not only was this journey remarkable for the tenacity of the crew, who spent 16 days on the crossing, but for the feat of navigation by Frank Worsley, the captain of the *Endurance*. South Georgia's barely explored and uninhabited southern coast was reached, the landing proving as fraught as the crossing. Shackleton, with two others, then had to cross the unexplored glacial heart of the island to reach the whaling station at Stromness. From there he set out to rescue those left on Elephant Island.

The journey of the *Endurance* and her crew was recorded by Frank Hurley, a brilliant photographer, whose shots helped the trip become a legend of survival against the odds. But it is rarely mentioned that *Endurance* was only half the expedition, the other half going to the Ross Sea in order to lay supply dumps for Shackleton's expected traverse. This expedition was far less successful, resulting in the deaths of three men. The supply dumps they prepared were also far from adequate and, had Shackleton succeeded in reaching the shores of the Weddell Sea, he would have been lucky to survive the traverse.

The world that Shackleton and his men returned to had changed, almost beyond their imagining. The

above

Pipe in hand, Frank Wild contemplates the wreck of the *Endurance*. One of Frank Hurley's remarkable series of photos of the expedition.

below

Shackleton, Peary and Amundsen. On 16 November 1913 the three greatest polar explorers of the age were entertained at the Bellevue Stratford Hotel, Philadelphia.

war which would be 'over by Christmas' was grinding on. Shackleton's reception was less rapturous than the one his name now elicits: on the Falklands one islander commented that he should have 'been at the war long ago instead of messing about on icebergs'. Back in Britain his men were called up for active service: Tim McCarthy, who had survived the open boat journey, was killed within four months of reaching South Georgia. Shackleton, too old for active service, was now something of an anachronism. In 1920 he decided to go south again. He had no clear objective: perhaps he just wanted to be in a place where he felt less out of touch. At South Georgia he had a massive heart attack and died.

After Shackleton's trip, journeys to the Antarctic were mainly to fill in the gaps in the map of the continent. It soon became apparent that using planes speeded this process, and also allowed a new generation to adventure among the frozen wastes. Englishman Hubert Wilkins and American Ben Eielson made the first Antarctic flight from Deception Island in 1928, the first flight over the continent itself being the following year, from the Little America base at the Bay of Whales, by Richard Byrd and his pilot Bernt Balchen. Byrd, whose claim to have been the first man to fly to the North Pole has since been discredited, then made the first flight over the South Pole. In 1933 Byrd returned with an even bigger expedition, his planes exploring a vast tract of Antarctica, though the expedition was chiefly notable for Byrd's decision to overwinter alone in a hut inland from his base. This feat of solitary endurance almost ended in disaster when fumes from a faulty petrol-driven generator poisoned him. Alarmed by his increasingly erratic radio messages the base team mounted a rescue, arriving just in time to save his life.

The next flyer on the continent was Lincoln Ellsworth, who had made Arctic flights with Amundsen and Nobile. Ellsworth came south in 1933 determined to add a trans-Antarctic flight to his Arctic record. He

above
Ellsworth's plane *Polar Star* slipping through the ice after being unloaded from his ship (the *Wyatt Earp*) in 1933. The anticipated flights had to be abandoned.

was unsuccessful in 1933 and again in 1934 (when, during the journey home his ship was overrun by rats which not only ate all the expedition's boats and snowshoe webbing but also killed and ate the ship's cat). In 1935 he tried again, this time succeeding in flying the length of the Antarctic Peninsula and on to the Ross Sea.

After the 1939-45 war, as part of the International Geographical Year (IGY) the Americans set up a base at the South Pole, one which remains to this day. On 31 October 1956 a DC3 landed at the Pole and Admiral George Dufek became the eleventh man, and the first American, to stand there. As part of the IGY the British decided to realise Shackleton's dream of crossing Antarctica from the Weddell to the Ross. In charge of the project was Vivian Fuchs who was to lead a team from the Weddell to the Ross, using supply depots beyond the Pole, laid down by a New Zealand team under Sir Edmund Hillary who, three years earlier, had, with Tenzing Norgay, been first to Everest's summit. The Fuchs team overwintered on the shores of the Weddell in 1956, Hillary's team using part of the winter to repeat the 'Worst Journey in the World' to test his vehicles.

Fuchs's team found the going difficult, especially getting his vehicles on to the plateau, but once established there things went better, his US SnoCats performing well. On the other side of the continent

right
Ed Hillary's vehicles for the Trans-Antarctic expedition were standard Ferguson tractors with added tracks and a modified cab. Here Hillary tries out a standard, but trackless, tractor in New Zealand prior to the trip. His team, presumably gathered (in expedition clothing) to be impressed by the demonstration, appear either baffled or completely underwhelmed.

Hillary laid down his depots and then waited for Fuchs, the plan being that he would lead him to the Ross-side base. With Fuchs behind schedule Hillary decided to press on, and on 4 January 1958 his team reached the Pole, the first men to do so overland since Scott in 1912. This journey caused considerable friction between Hillary and Fuchs, the latter believing (almost certainly correctly) that it was an attempt to steal his thunder. However, the argument, which even reached prime ministerial level, did not stop Hillary returning to the Pole to join in the welcome for Fuchs when his team finally arrived two weeks later. Fuchs then continued along Hillary's outward route, accomplishing the first Antarctic traverse in March.

In 1980 the Trans-Globe expedition, the three-man British team of Charles Burton (whose death at the age of 59 was announced as this book was being written), Sir Ranulph Fiennes and Oliver Sheppard (none with Antarctic experience) landed on the Queen Maud Land coast, close to the 0° meridian. The expedition was intending to circumnavigate the earth along (or as close as possible to) the prime meridian and, as part of that trip, was intending to cross Antarctica using open snow scooters, a feat which many claimed was not possible because of the extremes of cold and wind the continent experiences. Despite the cold the men succeeded, reaching the Pole on 15 December and Scott base on Ross Island on 11 January 1981. They had achieved the second crossing of the continent, covering 4,200 kms (2,600 miles) in 66 days.

The next land journey to the Pole, in 1985–86, recreated the journey of Scott's team. 'In the Footsteps of Scott' was the brainchild of Briton Robert Swan and was intended to reproduce, as far as possible, Scott's journey, Swan even transporting his team to the start by ship. The team recreated the 'Worst Journey in the World' by manhauling to Cape Crozier, then, almost exactly duplicating Scott's route, three men – Swan with Roger Mear and Gareth Wood – set off for the Pole. They took no radio so as to recreate the same sense of isolation, but had sledges that weighed only half as much – in part because they were not walking out (they had their own air transport), in part because modern foodstuffs and equipment are lighter. Having set out on the same date as Scott they arrived at the Pole on 11 January 1986, a week ahead of Scott's schedule. In another parallel with Scott's trip they arrived to bad news: their ship had sunk. To make matters worse they also had a hostile reception from the Americans, much as several later expeditions have done. Officially this is because the Americans fear having to risk men and resources rescuing idiot adventurers, but it is difficult not to see an element of proprietorial rights in the antagonism.

The 'Footsteps' expedition was the last which used a ship for transport (though the use of a ship was a choice rather than a necessity). The air age had truly arrived with the discovery, at Patriot Hills near

above top
Hillary (left) and Fuchs (right) are greeted at the South Pole by Admiral George Dufek.

above
British explorers Ranulph Fiennes (left) and Charles Burton tidying up the Trans-Globeship before a ceremony to mark the end of the three years, 56,000 km (35,000 miles) expedition. Sadly Charles Burton's death was announced while this book was in preparation.

the south-western edge of the Ronne Ice Shelf, of a natural blue-ice runway which could be used safely by wheeled (as opposed to ski-mounted) aircraft. Using this base, and then a light aircraft to fly to the shore of the Weddell Sea, Reinhold Messner, the world's greatest high-altitude climber, and the German Arved Fuchs repeated the British traverse by Vivian Fuchs (no relation to Arved), using specially designed parawings to assist with the towing of their sledges. This was the first non-mechanical traverse, Shackleton's dream if not his method.

At Patriot Hills, Messner and Fuchs met the team which was making the longest traverse possible on Antarctica. The six-man team – American Will Steger, Frenchman Jean-Louis Etienne, Victor Boyarsky, a Russian scientist, Qin Dahe, a Chinese glaciologist, and two dog experts, the Japanese Keizo Funatsu and Briton Geoff Somers – started near the tip of the Antarctic Peninsula, reached the pole and continued to the Russian Mirny Station on the shore of the Davis Sea, a distance of 6,000 km (3,725 miles) using dog sledges and moving between a dozen previously laid-down supply depots as well as being re-supplied by air from Patriot Hills.

Despite these successes, the idea of an unsupported traverse of the continent remained elusive, having been attempted several times (including a couple of near misses by Briton Ranulf Fiennes and his partners). One target was achieved in 1993–94 when the Norwegian Erling Kagge made the first unsupported, solo journey to the Pole from Berkner Island. Not until three years later was the first unsupported traverse achieved by another Norwegian, Børge Ousland, the outstanding polar explorer of the age. Since that time there have been other traverses, each lengthening the traverse line, until in the austral summer of 2000–2001 the Norwegians Rolf Bae and Eirik Sønneland completed a distance of 3,800 kms (2,360 miles), the longest unsupported journey ever made. The pair started out from Queen Maud, trekking for 105 days to reach McMurdo base – a phenomenal achievement but one which the lure of the southern continent will doubtless see surpassed at some future time.

Peaks

When man began to climb mountains is a question to which there are several answers depending upon how the word 'climb' is defined. The discovery of 'Oetzi', the Copper Age hunter, high in the Alps implies that men were certainly going into the mountains over 5,000 years ago: but that was a search for food which involved a climb. And the soldiers of Alexander needed to climb the Sogdian Rock in 327BC in order to force the ascent and inflict defeat on Oxyartes. In 1280 Peter III, King of Aragon, climbed Canigou, the prominent peak at the eastern end of the Pyrenees. His ascent does at least have the merits of having been completed for no better reason than Canigou being claimed the highest peak in his realm. Sadly, the fact that the king said he found a lake on the summit, one in which a dragon lived, implies that his ascent owed more to fervent desire than actuality, especially as the idea that dragons lived on mountain tops was one that was widely believed.

Half a century later, in 1336, the poet Petrarch climbed Mont Ventoux and then wrote about the climb and the summit view in a lyrical passage that has hardly been bettered as an expression of the aesthetic joy of climbing.

In the same century several other peaks were climbed, some for scientific reasons, but many for reasons that had more to do with satisfying the human spirit than with any purely practical idea. Evidence of this was found in the grim discovery of the frozen corpses of children, close to the summit of Llullaillaco, a 6,723m (22,713 ft) mountain in northern Argentina: the three children are believed to have been human sacrifices by the Inca priesthood, perhaps 500 years ago.

And now, in the 21st century, Mount Kailas is still regarded as a sacred mountain by the Tibetans. There is something about mountains which touches the need for spirituality in many human beings and inspires the need to reach their summits in many more.

The Eiger was finally climbed in 1938 by the Germans Anderl Heckmair, Ludwig Vörg and Heinrich Harrer, and the Austrian Fritz Kasperak. Even that ascent was not without controversy. Adolf Hitler saw the climb as a triumph of the Germanic peoples and met the climbers. The argument over whether the climb was inspired by nationalism has never gone away and was brought into sharp focus by revelations about Harrer's past when the film of his book *Seven Years in Tibet* was released a few years ago. The face was not climbed again until 1947, and had had only 50 ascents by the mid-1960s. As an interesting statistic, the fiftieth climb was by a woman, Daisy Voog, the first female ascent. Interspersed with the successful ascent were more tragedies, all played out in front of the Scheidegg telescope. Worst of all perhaps was that in 1957, when an Italian was left hanging from ropes and two young Germans disappeared. A second Italian was rescued from the face, and that rescue and the lonely death of his partner again made for headline news and ghoulish watching.

The Eiger has continued to play a prominent role in the development of the Alps, despite the standard route now being considered one of the easiest climbs on the vast wall (though caution is required when suggesting as much; easiest should not be read as 'easy': when the weather turns bad, it is still a major undertaking and the death toll continues to mount). The level of difficulty achieved by those at the top of the sport has, of course, been pushed upwards, though it is now chiefly climbers rather than newspaper readers who recognise the latest hard lines. Yet, it is the peaks of the great north faces which attract attention. In 1952 the west face of the Dru was climbed by a French team. Then in 1955 the Italian Walter Bonatti achieved what is widely believed to be the greatest feat of Alpine mountaineering by soloing a new route on the Dru. In 1965 he celebrated the centenary of the Matterhorn's first ascent by soloing a new route on the north face, this time in winter. Further advances were made on the Eiger (International team, 1966), Direct Grandes Jorasses (René Desmaisson, The Shroud, 1968) and on the Dru (Cecchinel/Jaeger, 1973 and Destivelle, 1991).

Today's climbers, though pushing standards even further, have also returned to the great faces to reduce the amount of aid used, climbing the old routes in the new style. They have also brought the techniques acquired in the Alps to the world's greater ranges. In 1954 a French team pushed a route up the imposing south face of Aconcagua, and then in 1985 the Pole Wojciech Kurtyka and the German Robert Schauer climbed the west face of Gasherbrum IV in the Karakoram. This, and the route on the north face of Thalay Sagar in the Garwhal Himal by the Hungarians Dékàny and Ozvàth, are regarded by most experts as the finest high-altitude climbs to have been accomplished to date.

opposite
Lynn Hill laybacking beneath the Great Roof on El
Capitan's Nose in 1993. With the British climber Simon
Nadin, Lynn almost completed the first free ascent of this
famous climb, the pair having to finish the last few
pitches of the route using aid when they ran out of food.
Lynn returned a short while later with American climber
Brooke Sandahl and completed the climb. Each of these
climbs had taken several days. Later, Lynn repeated the
climb with American Steve Sutton in a single day. The
free ascent of the Great Roof has one of the main
challenges on the climb. Lynn is laybacking, a technique
which uses hands and feet in opposition.

ON THE ROCKS

Many of the advances used to improve standards
in the Alps were developed in rock climbing, a
sport which differs from alpinism in the scale of
the faces being climbed. Pure rock climbers may
take as long on a 30m (98 ft) route as their alpine
counterparts do on a great north face. In the USA's
Yosemite Valley the two ideas blended together
with the development of techniques which
allowed the vast, sheer faces of granite found
there to be climbed. The first major climb was in
1950 on Sentinel Rock, but the most famous such
climb was the ascent of the Nose on El Capitan
by Warren Harding's team in 1958. The climb took
45 days over an 18-month period and involved the
use of 675 pitons and 125 expansion bolts.

Other faces were climbed, newer generations
of climbers not only doing their own routes, but
attempting to reduce the amount of aid on the older
climbs. It soon became the norm to do climbs such
as the Nose in one push. The time to climb the
route tumbled. In 1975 it was done in a day. By
2001 this had been reduced to less than four hours.

At the same time as climbers were trying to reduce the time, others were trying to climb the route free –
that is with no artificial aids. This was finally achieved by Lynn Hill and Brooke Sandahl over two days in
1993. Lynn Hill later returned to establish another milestone by completing a free ascent in one day.

The techniques the Americans learned on the great Yosemite faces were transferred to Europe, a
four-man team climbing the south face of the Fou in 1963. Not that the Europeans were far behind in
terms of rock-climbing ability, or in the speed with which they acquired the new techniques. In Britain,
after the 1939–45 war rock climbing standards were advanced by a generation of rock climbers whose
roots were in the working class of northern England rather than in the university class that had dominated
the pre-war sport. Joe Brown and Don Whillans led the advance, Whillans later transferring his skills
to the Himalayas. Brown dominated British rock climbing for two decades, an unprecedented reign in so
competitive a sport.

In rock climbing, the turn-over at the top is similar to that in pop music, a comparison that seemed

below
Rebecca Stephens, the
first British woman to
climb Everest, and the
first British woman (and
third woman) to complete
the Seven Summits.

above
The first three women to
reach the summit of
Everest. On the right, the
Japanese Junko Tabei
who was the first
woman to do so on 16
May 1975, climbing from
Nepal (she was also the
first woman to climb the
Seven Summits). In the
centre, the Tibetan
Phantog who reached
the summit 11 days later
from Tibet. To the left is
Wanda Rutkiewicz who
reached the summit in
1978. Rutkiewicz, who
died on Kangchenjunga,
still holds the record for
female ascents of
8,000m peaks.

Swiss failing to notch up the second ascent.
Mme Kogan died on Cho Oyu in 1959 when
leading an all-women's expedition in an attempt
to repeat the climb. Not until 1974 did a woman
stand on the summit of an 8,000m (26,246 ft)
peak when a Japanese team climbed Manaslu.
The following year the Japanese Junko Tabei
climbed Everest by the South Col route, beating
by 11 days a Tibetan woman, Phantog, who
climbed from the north side. That same year, the
Polish woman Wanda Rutkiewicz led a team
which climbed Gasherbrum III, 7,952m (26,089 ft),
the highest peak to have had a first ascent by a
woman. Rutkiewicz led a women's team up the Matterhorn's north face in winter in 1978, then set out to
be the first woman to climb all fourteen 8,000m peaks. As this feat had been achieved only by a handful
of men at the time, women were now competing at the pinnacle of the sport. Rutkiewicz climbed eight
8,000m peaks (including Everest, third female ascent, and K2, first female ascent) before disappearing on
Kangchenjunga. In terms of 8,000m ascents, she is still the most successful high altitude woman climber.
Rebecca Stephens became the first British woman to climb Everest in 1993 while in 1995 another Briton,
Alison Hargreaves, became the first woman to have made a confirmed ascent of Everest without bottled
oxygen (there having been a disputed climb in 1988).

At lower altitudes women are also now competing with men at the highest levels. Catherine
Destivelle's ascent of a new route on the Dru has already been mentioned. The French woman also made
the first repeat of Bonatti's Matterhorn north face route, solo and in winter. In Britain she soloed the Old
Man of Hoy, not the country's hardest climb, but a very spectacular sea stack. Then, in 1993, American

woman Lynn Hill achieved a climb which was coveted by, but had defeated, many top male climbers, making the first free (i.e. aid-less) ascent of the Nose on Yosemite's El Capitan.

THE GREAT RANGES

At the end of the 19th century – indeed, almost from the end of the Golden Age of Alpine climbing – climbers began to look further afield for unclimbed peaks. Freshfield headed towards the Caucasus. In Africa the German Ludwig Purtscheller climbed Kilimanjaro, while the Briton Harold Mackinder climbed Mount Kenya, in 1899, a climb which involved the bashing of a trail through primeval forest; this was not repeated for 30 years when another British team, including Eric Shipton and Wyn Harris, braved the same approach.

In New Zealand, attempts to climb Mount Cook began in 1882, but it was not until 1894, after numerous failures, that a team of young New Zealanders – Tom Fyfe, Jack Clarke and George Graham – reached the top by a route which was not to be repeated for more than 60 years. This local team had been spurred to make the ascent by the arrival of the experienced Briton Edward Fitzgerald and his guide, Matthias Zurbriggen. Fitzgerald was miffed by the locals' having made the climb and declined to make

right

An aerial photograph of Mount Cook from the south, over the Hooker Valley. Taken in winter, the shot shows the formidable nature of the peak. A few years ago a rock fall from the summit altered the height a little. Sadly it did not add to it – Mount Cook would have been a fine addition to the list of continental summits, a more worthy candidate than Kosciusko or even the Carstenz Pyramid.

a second ascent. Zurbriggen was less bothered and soloed a different, far easier route.

Fitzgerald and Zurbriggen moved on to South America, though they were following in the footsteps of Whymper who had already visited the continent, climbing Chimborazo in 1880. Fitzgerald and Zurbriggen wanted Aconcagua, the highest peak. In 1897 they succeeded, though again it was only Zurbriggen who reached the top. Much later, the high-angled ice slopes of the Andean peaks, and the sheer rock peaks of Patagonia were to attract the attention of the world's great climbers. In 1951 Lionel Terray led a team in the first ascent of Huantsan, while the same year also saw the first ascent of Alpamayo which many claim to be the most beautiful mountain the world. (The other main claimant for this title is Siniolchu in Sikkim, but everyone will have their own contender.) Terray was back in 1952, climbing Fitzroy, the highest of the Patagonian peaks, with Guido Magnone as part of a French team. Later Terray claimed that the climbing of Cerro Torre, next to Fitzroy, was the greatest mountaineering feat of all time. In fact it has also become the most controversial.

In 1959 a three-man team camped below the peak. One man soon abandoned the attempt, but the other two continued. One was Cesare Maestri, the leading Italian climber of his day, a master rock climber whose abilities and solo ascents were comparable with those of Hermann Buhl. The other was the Austrian Toni Egger. Days later Maestri returned alone, claiming to have reached the summit with Egger but to have descended alone after Egger was swept away by an avalanche. Inconsistencies in his account of the climb, and later attempts on the peak raised doubts as to the validity of Maestri's claim. Outraged by the doubters Maestri returned to Cerro Torre, using a 60kg (132 lb) compressed-air gun to slam bolts into the rock which he used to climb to the mushroom of ice which surmounts the summit. This he could not climb. It was now the turn of the rest of the climbing world to be outraged, especially as Maestri had left the compressor hanging from a bolt near the top of the peak. Subsequently Cerro Torre has been climbed several times, one climb over the line of Maestri's claimed irst route merely adding to the initial doubts. However, Maestri has never changed his story and remains defiant.

THE HIGHEST PEAKS

For many the only great range is the Himalaya/Karakoram where the world's highest mountains are congregated. Exploration of these began with the surveyors of British India, several claims being made of heights reached during the last years of the 19th century. The first true expedition was that of Albert Mummery, the foremost British mountaineer of his era, a man who embraced the modern approach, climbing hard routes for the joy of doing it rather than to reach a summit. With two other pioneering Britons, Norman Collie and Geoffrey Hastings, and two Gurkhas, Mummery set off to climb Nanga Parbat in 1895. Mummery and the two Gurkhas disappeared after abandoning an attempt on the Diamir face, probably killed by an avalanche as they attempted to cross the Diamir Pass. In 1907 another Briton, Tom Longstaff, together with two French guides, the Brocherel brothers, reached the summit of Trisul (7,120m / 23,359 ft), surpassing Zurbriggen's ascent of Aconcagua as the highest summit to have been reached. This record was broken by the 1930 International Expedition (led by the Swiss Günther Dyhrenfurth) which climbed Jonsong (7,420m / 24,343 ft). The new record stood for just one year, until the British climbed Kamet (7,756m / 25,446 ft). Eric Shipton and Frank Smythe were among those who reached the top. The summit height record was increased again in 1936 when Bill Tilman and Noel Odell, members of an Anglo–American

below
The only known photograph of Albert Mummery climbing. It was taken by Lily Bristow, a noted woman climber whose partnership with Mummery ended abruptly, probably because Mummery's wife became nervous of the relationship.

far right
Dr Tom Longstaff. Longstaff was a qualified doctor, rich enough not to have to practise, who spent years exploring the Himalaya where 'his pirate beard blazed red against the Himalaya snows' according to one companion. Longstaff's climb of Trisul was the highest summit reached for over 20 years.

above

Holdsworth on the
summit of Kamet. As
with the other members
of the British team he is
only referred to by
surname throughout the
book on the expedition.
On the pre-climb photo,
Holdsworth has his pipe
clenched between his
teeth. On the summit it
is still there.

right

Nanda Devi from the
south. The mountain is
among the most
beautiful in the world. It
is also one of the most
difficult to approach,
requiring a difficult walk
through the Rishi Gorge
to reach an inner
sanctuary above which
the peak rises. This shot
was taken by Tilman
during the 1936
expedition.

team, reached the summit of Nanda Devi (7,816m / 25,643 ft). After the 1939–45 war, the French climbed Annapurna (8,047m / 26,400 ft) in 1950, before the British claimed the highest peak of all in 1953.

In terms of height reached, the peak records from 1907 onwards were rendered irrelevant by the early British expeditions to Everest. The first of these was in 1921, led by Charles Howard-Bury and including George Mallory, whose name has become inextricably linked with the peak. Unable to go through Nepal, at that time closed to outsiders, the British used their influence with Tibet to approach the north side of the mountain. The team reached the North Col before being forced back by bad weather. In 1922 the British returned, passing the 8,000m (26,246 ft) contour for the first time. George Finch and Geoffrey Bruce finally reached a height of 8,320m (27,296 ft), but the expedition was marred by the death of seven Sherpas in an avalanche. In 1924 the third expedition pushed the achieved height record to 8,570m (28,116 ft), Edward Norton reaching this height alone after his companion, Howard Somervell, was forced to abandon his attempt due to high-altitude cough. But it is not for that record altitude that the 1924 expedition is remembered. A few days after Norton's attempt, a final climb was made by Mallory and

left

Mallory and Norton at their high point in 1922. Although the record for the highest peak attained increased steadily throughout the first half of the 20th century, finally going beyond 8,000 m for the first time in 1950 with the ascent of Annapurna, the heights reached by the Everest expeditions of the 1920s overtopped all summits except Everest itself. Mallory and Norton, together with Somervell, were the first to cross the 8,000 m contour, eventually reaching 8,200 m (26,900 ft). A few days later, Finch and Geoffrey Bruce reached 8,320 m (27,300 ft). Not only was this the highest point reached on the 1922 expedition, but it was also memorable as it was Bruce's first ever climb.

Sandy Irvine. The pair set out from the last camp on 8 June and were seen around midday by Noel Odell as he climbed up to support them. They were never again seen alive.

The finding of Mallory's body in 1999 answers one question that had been discussed ever since the disappearance and, more importantly, the discovery of Irvine's axe in 1933. Mallory still had a rope attached to his waist so the pair had definitely been climbing together when an accident occurred. It is conjectured from the site of the body that they were climbing down, something which accords with the position of the axe which was below the point at which Odell last saw the pair. The axe could have marked the point where an accident occurred, perhaps falling from Irvine's hand when he was startled by Mallory's fall. But these considerations do not answer the fundamental question – if the pair were indeed climbing down, as now seems indisputable, from where were they coming? Odell's sighting is crucial here, but over the years his opinion of where he saw the pair changed. At first he said it had been at or above the Second Step, the formidable obstacle that occupied the Chinese for several hours during the first known ascent of the north side of Everest. If Odell was correct then the summit might well have been reached. Later Odell changed his mind, believing his sighting was of the pair when they were much

right
The formidable South
Face of Aconcagua
viewed from the
Horcones Valley. The
valley curves around the
western flank of the
peak and is followed by
the 'standard' route
which then ascends the
north-west/north side.
The South Face was
climbed by a French
team led by Réné Ferlet
in 1954, the climb
requiring six camps on
the face. The face is
both difficult and very
dangerous and is rarely
climbed.

ACONCAGUA

The highest peak in South America is, at 6,960m (22,835 ft), also the second highest of the seven summits. It was first climbed in 1896 when Edward Fitzgerald led a team that included Matthias Zurbriggen, the famous alpine guide. The team climbed the now-standard route – from the Horcones Valley and up the western side of the peak – but the summit was reached by Zurbriggen alone when the rest of the party were laid low with altitude problems. Later other members of the team did reach the summit, but sadly Fitzgerald was not one of them.

In 1934 a Polish team explored the eastern side of the mountain, making a route up what is now called the Polish Glacier. In the 1950s the mountain's south face, a vast expanse of ice and rock, attracted the attention of many of the world's best climbers. It was finally climbed by a French team in 1954. A variation on this route was climbed in 1974 by Reinhold Messner.

Today the mountain has as many as 1,500 ascents each year, though as many climbers again succumb to bad weather – the mountain is notorious for the *viento blanco*, the white wind, which reduces visibility and threatens to blow all and everything off the hill – or altitude problems.

McKINLEY

Though the National Park which now surrounds North America's highest peak (6,194m / 20,321 ft) has

right and below
Mount McKinley, the
highest peak in North
America. The peak
stands in the Denali
National Park in central
Alaska. The upper
photograph was taken
from the Eielson Visitor
Centre. The Centre
(named for one of
Alaska's most famous
bush pilots) lies on the
road which penetrates
deep into the Park.
Visitors cannot drive
along it, but must take
the Park bus. From the
Centre the mountain
rears above the Muldrow
Glacier and shows the
double summit structure
distinctly. The right-hand
(north) summit is that
climbed (or claimed) by
the 'Sourdough'
expedition of 1910. The
left-hand (south) summit
– the true summit – was
climbed in 1913.

In the lower photo-
graph, sunset lights up
McKinley's northern
face. The shot was taken
from Wonder Lake, the
most remote camp site
in the Denali National
Park, one with limited
sites which must be
booked weeks in
advance during the
summer months. The
camper is at the heart of
the Park, with
outstanding views of the
mountain, but is
tormented by millions of
mosquitoes.

VINSON

Until 1957 the highest peak in Antarctica (at 4,897m / 16,066 ft) was undiscovered. In that year it was first seen from the air, though it was not until the area had been surveyed that it was realised that it was indeed the highest. It was then named, by the Americans, for Senator Carl Vinson who had done much to persuade the US government to support Antarctic exploration. It was climbed, in 1966, by the first team to attempt it, Pete Schoening (who had also been in the first party to climb Gasherbrum I), Barry Corbett, John Evans and Bill Long. Most climbers follow the route of the first ascent, but several other routes exist – most notable, one forged by a Slovenian team. The climbing is straightforward, but the local climate is, unsurprisingly, both cold and windswept. Rather more of a problem for aspirant seven summiters is extreme cost, Antarctica being a very expensive place to reach. With access strictly controlled, aspiring climbers are forced into one of a small number of travel possibilities, each of which involves serious expense.

right
Mount Vinson viewed from Mount Shinn top the south. The standard route starts from the bottom right of the photograph, following the ridge and then then plateau edge to the summit.

CARSTENZ, OR KOSCIUSKO

When Dick Bass completed his seven summits in 1985 his list included Mount Kosciusko (2,228m / 7,309 ft) in Australia, a peak named for a Polish hero, after the man who had made the first known ascent, Sir Paul Strzelecki, noted the similarity between its shape and that of the tomb of Tadeusz Kosciusko in Cracow Cathedral. It is very likely that Aborigines had reached the summit earlier, perhaps centuries earlier. Kosciucsko's summit has been reached by bicycle, that fact alone probably prejudicing the climbing world against it. This led Pat Morrow, a Canadian who had been in quiet competition with Bass for the seven summits, to look for a more fitting choice.

With support from geographers, Morrow extended the Australian continent to include adjacent islands

below

The Carstenz Pyramid. The standard route to the top is a rock climb up the water-worn, but excellent limestone of the peak's north face. The exotic position of the peak add to the joys of the climb, but the expense of reaching such a remote area mean that Carstenz is unlikely to become a popular destination for climbers who are not seeking the Seven Summits.

(Australasia or Oceania) and as a result saw the Carstenz Pyramid on West Papua (formerly Irian Jaya) as the seventh peak. Though claimed to have been seen by the Dutchman Jan Carstenz in about 1623, the peak was not actually proved to exist until the early 20th century when a British expedition hacked a way through the jungle to its base. A Dutch geographical expedition failed to climb the peak in 1936 and it was then left alone until 1961 when a further attempt failed. In the following year Heinrich Harrer, veteran of the Eiger north face, succeeded in leading a team to the top along what is now the standard route. Reinhold Messner added another route on the second ascent, while later climbers have made several more on the peak's north face. For climbers the expense of reaching West Papua is offset both by the climbing and by the chance to visit the people of the Dani tribe. Harrer's book on his expedition was called *I Come from the Stone Age*, a title which correctly reflected the Dani. It is not much changed today: Dani men still wear the *koteka* or penis gourd (and little else besides) despite the strenuous efforts of the authorities during Operation Koteka to impose a more 'modern' form of dress. It is claimed that when the first consignment of shorts were airlifted in at the start of the campaign the bemused Dani wore them as hats.

'Few moments of exhilaration can come as that which stands at the threshold of wild travel,' Gertrude Bell wrote. The knowledge and associations she had developed whilst travelling throughout Persia, Iraq and Syria lead her to become one of the most powerful women in the British Empire. She was later to be integral to the creation of Iraq, where she became one of King Faisal's closest advisers. 'I don't care to be in London much. I like Baghdad, and I like Iraq. It's the real East and it's stirring; things are happening here, and the romance of it all touches me and absorbs me.' This photo shows Bell's tent at camp in Urzeh, Iraq.

World War I and was the only woman to be employed in the Intelligence Service there. This relationship continued after the war and Bell was instrumental in the creation of the new Iraqi nation and its political identity. For many years, she was a close adviser to its first ruler, King Faisal. She developed such an understanding and knowledge of the desert that she was awarded the Royal Geographical Society's Gold Medal for Exploration. Her personal life, however, was not so smooth, and Bell committed suicide in Baghdad in 1926.

This area was further opened up to the western mind by the journeys and

below

Bell hated any form of publicity or 'advertisement' as she called it and wrote home: 'Please, please don't supply information about me or photographs of me to newspaper correspondents … I hate the whole advertisement business. I always throw all letters (fortunately they're not many in number) asking for an interview or a photograph straight in the wastepaper basket.'

right

'It is, I believe, a fallacy to think of travellers' qualities as physical. If I had to write a decalogue for journeys, eight out of ten virtues should be moral, and I should put first of all a temper as serene at the end as at the beginning of the day. Then would come the capacity to accept values and to judge by standards other than our own. The rapid judgment of character; and a love of nature, which must include human nature also. The power to disassociate oneself from one's own bodily sensations. A knowledge of the local history and language. A leisurely and uncensorious mind. A tolerable constitution and the capacity to eat and sleep at any moment. And lastly, and especially here, a quickness in repartee.'
The Southern Gates of Arabia, Freya Stark.

writings of Freya Madeline Stark. Attracted to the 'blank spots' on maps of the Middle East, Stark was drawn to the 'lure of exploration' as she called it, and was to retain this wandering spirit until her late eighties, searching both for archaeological ruins and a sense of change and contrast:

'If I were asked the most agreeable thing in life, I should say it is the pleasure of contrast. One cannot imagine anyone but an angel sitting with a harp in Paradise forever. The ordinary human being needs a change. This is the secret charm of the oasis, usually an indifferent patch of greenery made precious solely by surrounding sands.'

She moved to San Remo, Italy in 1921, where she learnt Arabic from a monk, on her premise that the

Livingstone continued to fight against the slave trade and lobbied the Portuguese king into agreeing to cooperate. However, Portuguese officers ignored his directions and in 1864 the expedition was recalled as a result of both Portuguese pressure and financial considerations.

LIVINGSTONE AND THE NILE

Shortly after returning to Britain, Livingstone set out again to play his part in the debate that was then raging over the mystery of the Nile. Following the death of Speke, Livingstone was hired by the RGS to settle the matter once and for all. Landing at the mouth of the Rovuma, in Portuguese territory, his party travelled north-west via Lake Nyasa to Lake Tanganyika, discovering Lake Mweru and its effluent, the Lualaba River, which he believed was the Nile. Unfriendly Arab traders thwarted him in his attempt to follow the Lualaba downstream, and he returned to Ujiji weakened, both mentally and physically. Livingstone had spent six years on this particular journey, a journey he expected to have completed much more rapidly. By 1871 Europe had not heard from him for some time and rumours of his death had started to circulate.

Such was the interest in Livingstone's whereabouts that Henry Morton Stanley, a young Welsh-born American journalist, travelled to Africa in search of him. Sent there by his employer James Gordon Bennett, the proprietor of the *New York Herald*, Stanley was effectively given a blank cheque to get the story, a story that would bring enormous publicity to the newspaper. The legendary meeting between Livingstone and Stanley took place on the shores of Lake Tanganyika, and Stanley's famous words came about as a result of his inability to judge how to greet such a man, in such a situation, and in such a place:

'I would have run to him, only I was a coward in the presence of such a mob – would have embraced him, only, he being an Englishman, I did not know how he would receive me; so I did what cowardice and false pride suggested was the best thing – walked deliberately to him, took off my hat and said…'

'Dr Livingstone, I presume?' was his greeting to a tired and jaded man. Yet, in Stanley's presence, Livingstone rediscovered his energy. They explored the northern end of Lake Tanganyika, establishing that what was thought to be the Nile was in fact the Ruizizi, and it flowed into the lake rather than out of it. Livingstone again turned to the Lualaba, convinced that at its source were the four fountains that Herodotus had claimed and that it was a headwater of the Nile. Disregarding Stanley's attempts to make him return to England because of his ill-health, Livingstone left Stanley at Kazeh in March 1872 and travelled to Lake Bangweulu to try to prove his theory. Increasingly ill and suffering repeated haemorrhages, Livingstone died in May 1873, as he knelt at the foot of his bed. Chuma and Susi, his devoted companions, buried his heart and organs by a tree on which they engraved his name. Then, embalmed in salt and alcohol, he was carried to Zanzibar and taken home to be buried in Westminster Abbey the following year.

Undeterred, Stanley took on the task of navigating the Lualaba, financed now by the proprietors of the *New York Herald* and *The Daily Telegraph*. His route passed through Lake Victoria and the Kingdom of Buganda – which Speke and Grant had visited a decade previously. They then travelled south to Lake Tanganyika, and the circumnavigation of the lake proved it had no relationship with the Nile. The only outlet was the Lukuga River, which fed the Lualaba. On his expedition to follow the course of this river, Stanley's party fought 34 battles with people on the banks of the river or in canoes, and navigated rapids and falls. At the final test, the Livingstone (or Stanley) Falls, where the river descends 300m (984 ft) over 32 cataracts, the last European man in the party (save Stanley) was drowned. One thousand days after the journey began, 114 men

out of an original party of 350 staggered out of the forest to the sea at Boma in Angola. Midway through their journey, Stanley had discovered the river was called the Congo, and he and Livingstone had been wrong – the Nile had no connection with the rivers to the south.

Stanley's Congo expedition, however, had not diminished his interest in the area, and he returned to England to generate support for the development of the region. With the Conservative administration uninterested in his propositions, Stanley was approached by King Leopold II of Belgium who founded the Association Internationale Africaine as a basis for his imperial designs on West Africa. By July 1879 Stanley was back in the Congo basin, building a railway and founding Leopoldville, which later became Kinshasa. His arrival beat the French who, led by Count Pierre Savorgnan de Brazza, were forced to the other bank and created Brazzaville, now capital city of the Congo.

Stanley was to return once more to the Congo on the Emin Pasha relief expedition in 1887. Emin was a German naturalist employed by the Egyptian government in their short-lived empire in southern Sudan. He had become cut off near Lake Albert during a Madhist uprising in 1881. The relief party came from the west coast via the Congo and the Aruwimi River rather than the more well-trodden road from the east, struggling through some of the densest forest on earth for five months. The forests were also home to tribes of pygmies who attacked them with poisoned arrows; as a result of these attacks and the harsh conditions, the death toll was extremely high. Emin Pasha, who was unconcerned at the position he was in, needed some persuasion to leave. He later returned and was killed there. It was during this return journey that Stanley glimpsed the Ruwenzori or the 'Mountains of the Moon', the legendary peaks that Ptolemy had written of so many centuries previously. His party traced its way around the mountains and discovered how their water fed the Semliki River and, henceforth, Lake Albert. The final piece of the

right

Stanley: 'Ruwenzori has been visible the last three days. That snow-covered range has been a most attractive and beautiful sight – pure, dazzling, varying in colours with the hours, with infinite depth of opaline blue all round it, until the sun set and dark night covered the earth … We have not much to boast of … the ancient travellers, geographers and authors had a very fair idea of whence the Nile issued … had heard of the Lunae Montes, and the triple lakes, and of the springs which gave birth to the famous river of Egypt.'

mystery had been put in place – the geography of the Nile sources was finally completed.

The race to claim territories in the Congo basin was the beginning of what came to be known as 'The Scramble'. In 1884, the Berlin Conference had been called to assess and even check the speed at which Europe was claiming Africa but, increasingly, exploratory motives were now much more based on political, rather than inquisitive and geographical desires. The Marchand Mission, for example, was a French attempt to prevent the British from claiming the Congo–Nile watershed, and Stanley attempted to win the valuable and respected service of Emin Pasha for the British. Despite Stanley's rescue, Pasha instead offered his services to Germany and was given the task of securing the territories south of and along Lake Victoria and up to Lake Albert.

SCHWEINFURTH AND THOMSON

Aside from the Nile quest, the African jungle was further explored during and after this period by Schweinfurth, Thomson and Kingsley. Between 1869 and 1871, Georg August Schweinfurth, a German botanist, explored more thoroughly the Bahr el Ghazl, the equatorial region south-west of the Nile. Primarily interested in hunting for plants, Schweinfurth was also fascinated, as were so many at that time, by stories of cannibals and pygmies. Though unknown to Europeans, the area was already well travelled by slave and ivory traders and was criss-crossed with their stations. On foot, he travelled through the jungle with these traders for protection, as their activity had made the native tribes highly suspicious and aggressive towards outsiders.

Accompanying the ivory traders, Schweinfurth ventured into areas reputed to be inhabited by cannibals, and became the first European to stand on the bank of the Uele River and the first European to meet the Akka pygmies. In exchange for his dog, he was given one pygmy, whom he hoped to take back to Germany with him, but Tikkitikki (as he had named him), reportedly died from overeating. Schweinfurth spent two and a half years in this region, from which he was to write *The Heart of Africa*, but unfortunately, on his return journey, all of his specimens and notes were lost in a camp fire. Without his tools, Schweinfurth apparently counted his steps back to Khartoum – all 1.25 million of them. Schweinfurth's health was to continue into his nineties and he went on to travel to Lebanon and Yemen and became the first European to explore parts of the Libyan Desert.

In 1882, while in Cairo, Schweinfurth received a visitor named Joseph Thomson. Thomson was a young geologist from Scotland, who had joined an RGS expedition to explore further the central African lakes. After the early death of the expedition's commander and as second-in-command, he took the lead. He took to entertaining the native people by removing his false teeth and dropping fruit salts which fizzed and popped in water. His first expedition to the north end of Lake Nyasa and further exploration of Lake Tanganyika proved

above

In 1897, French Captain Jean-Baptiste Marchand was in charge of an expedition aiming to explore the virtually unknown area of the Nile–Congo watershed. His objective was to establish a French presence from Fashoda in the east, 650 kms (410 miles) south of Khartoum to Libreville in the west, cutting off the British advance south. Upon reaching Fashoda, however, they were met by 20,000 of Kitchener's men who forced them to retreat. Marchand is pictured here in the centre.

Tom Mclean designed and helped build this 11 m (37 ft) bottle- shaped boat, the *Typhoo Atlantic Challenger*, which he sailed from New York to Falmouth, England in 1990 over 37 days. The boat was powered by a diesel engine and furnished with a four-poster bed, and raised money for the National Children's Homes charity, a charity particularly personal to McClean as he was an orphan himself.

below

Not content with rowing the Atlantic, in 1985, Tom McClean occupied Rockall to reaffirm Britain's claim on the small outcrop in the Atlantic. 450 km (280) miles west of the mainland, the 22 m (73 ft) high and 24 m (80 ft) wide rock has just one ledge of 3 m (10 ft) by 1.2 m (4 ft) near the summit. Mclean survived on this ledge for 40 days and nights in a unit of just 1.5 m by 1.2 m X 1.2 m (5 ft by 4 ft by 4 ft) that he designed himself. He also crossed the Atlantic in bottle-shaped and whale-shaped boats. McClean now runs an adventure centre on the west coast of Scotland.

radio, telex and a camera to film himself whilst rowing. What he was to encounter on his crossing would push him to the very limits of human endurance, both mental and physical. D'Aboville's departure had been delayed and as a result, he set off during one of the worst times of the year. Faced not only with the sheer physical challenge of rowing an average of 7,000 strokes per day, he was also faced with 12 m (40-foot) waves and 130-km (80-mile) per hour winds, culminating in a severe storm off the Oregon and Washington coast. His boat capsized 30 times, once for two hours where he was trapped inside, his oxygen depleting as he tried to right the boat. 134 days later, and almost three stone lighter, D'Aboville arrived at Illwaco, Washington.

left

In D'Aboville's account of his crossing, *Seul* (Alone), he discusses his attraction to the ocean and how, in crossing it and beating it, he went beyond the 'useful' drives and tasks of animals and achieved what only a human being could achieve: 'I have chosen the ocean as my field of confrontation, my field of battle, because the ocean is reality at its toughest, its most demanding. As my weapons against this awesome power, I have human values: intelligence, experience, and the stubborn will to win.'

right

In 1952, the French scientist, Dr Alain Bombard crossed the Atlantic in his rubber dinghy, *L'Hérétique*, (The Heretic) from the Canaries to Barbados. His aim was to prove that with no food or supplies, shipwrecked sailors could survive in an open boat living off the sea. During his 65-day crossing, he ate fish, plankton and seawater, losing 18 kg (three stone) as a result. He was awarded the Cross and Red Ribbon of the Legion of Honour by the French Minister of the Merchant Navy. The raft became compulsory cargo for all merchant and navy ships following his crossing. Bombard is pictured here on the right.

below

Thor Heyerdahl and Herman Watzinger chart the course of the *Kon-Tiki*, 28 December 1946 and so chart a course into history. There was by no means unanimous agreement over Norwegian Thor Heyerdahl's views on the origins of the Polynesian race and culture. To test his theory that they had originally come from the west and not the east as previously thought, he built a replica of an aboriginal balsa raft before setting out on a remarkable 101-day journey. Watzinger was Heyerdahl's second-in-command.

PROVING A THEORY – THOR HEYERDAHL

Thor Heyerdahl's motives for setting sail were altogether different from the other names in the story of man's understanding of the sea. Heyerdahl was a Norwegian zoologist, geographer and anthropologist who built three replicas of ancient sea craft in order to prove his migration theories.

Born in Larvik, Norway in 1914, Heyerdahl studied zoology and geography at university. As a student in 1937, he travelled to Tahiti with his wife Liv, where they studied the Polynesian culture and customs under the eye of the Supreme Polynesian Chief of Tahiti. They moved to the remote island of Fatu Hiva in the Marquesas Group, where they remained for a year, further studying the Polynesian customs and the origins of the island's plant life. His studies of plant life, prevailing winds and currents, and local legends and customs, pointed to the possibility that the island's inhabitants could have been settled from the east, from South America. Heyerdahl was to rock the scientific world and question established models with his theory that the islands had been settled in two waves, the first from Peru via Easter Island and the second via British Columbia. His theory was published in 1941 and more extensively in 1952 in his volume, *American Indians in the Pacific*.

Heyerdahl's work was met with strong resistance and scepticism from the geographical and anthropological communities, who maintained that migrants could not physically have travelled on their primitive craft. In 1947, to lend weight to his theory, Heyerdahl built a replica of the craft that South Americans used in ancient times. Despite a life-long fear of the ocean, he set sail from Callao, Peru with five other man on a boat named *Kon-Tiki*.

The *Kon-Tiki* consisted of a platform of 70 m² (750 ft²) with a cabin of bamboo and banana leaves, and two masts made of mangrove and was stocked up with native foods. Over 101 days they drifted 6,900 km (4,300 miles), adding

For most people the *Kon-Tiki* Expedition would have been enough excitement and adventure for one lifetime, but as Heyerdahl's research on ancient navigation continued, he became interested in reed boats made of papyrus. Again, conventional wisdom was that such craft would become waterlogged long before they were able to make substantial voyages. But in 1969 he constructed a vessel of ancient design from 12 tonnes of papyrus and, with a crew of seven, sailed *Ra* from Morocco some 4,350 km (2,700 miles) in 56 days until storms and problems with the construction forced them to abandon their attempt just seven days short of Barbados.

below

Spurred on by just missing his objective with the 15 m (49 ft) *Ra*, Heyerdahl was ready to repeat the voyage just 10 months later in the slightly smaller *Ra II*. Here they are shown setting off from Safi in Morocco, from where they sailed across the Atlantic at its widest part, completing the voyage to Barbados in just 57 days. Here was conclusive proof that simple vessels from the Mediterranean region could have crossed the Atlantic prior to Columbus – and how modern science had so underestimated ancient technology.

flying fish and plankton to their provisions. *Kon-Tiki* stayed afloat, and they arrived in Raroia in Polynesia, proving that the migration theory was possible. Heyerdahl wrote a book and made a film of the voyage, which won an Oscar for best documentary, captivating the public, but leaving many still sceptical. However, his later work found evidence of ancient navigation tools, increasing the acceptance of his views, and he began gradually to be taken more seriously.

Heyerdahl continued with his work on migration and ancient navigation, and in 1969, he built the *Ra*, a reed boat made of papyrus. The 15-metre (49 - foot) boat was launched from Safi, Morocco, and attempted to cross the Atlantic to show that boats could have been crossing the Atlantic prior to Columbus. With seven men from seven countries under the flag of the UN, the *Ra* was to sail 5000 km (3,125 miles), before being abandoned one week short of Barbados due to storms and construction problems. The following year, *Ra II* successfully crossed the widest part of the Atlantic (6,100km / 3800 miles) in 57 days, again proving that ancient vessels could make such a crossing.

In Iraq in 1977, Heyerdahl built the *Tigris*, this time aiming to show that civilisations in Mesopotamia, Egypt and the Indus Valley could have been in contact by sea. Wars in the area at the time prevented him from continuing, and he burnt the *Tigris* as an expression of anger at the political situation. Heyerdahl died at his home in Italy in 2001.

Underworlds

Even when the furthest shores and highest peaks had been identified, and in some cases reached or climbed, there remained frontiers as yet untouched by human exploration – the subterranean worlds of caves and the ocean floors.

It is thought that from earliest times man had used caves only for shelter, and so it is difficult to identify precisely the origins of caving purely for exploration. Shelter being the main consideration, early man was unlikely to have admired the underground world for its own sake – nevertheless, the painters at Lascaux, in France's Dordogne region, clearly penetrated further than was easy or necessary to find a place for their exquisite art, art that was created at least 15,000 years ago.

As recently as the 1970s a new tribe of people discovered in the Philippines were found to be living in caves but, in general, after man had learned to build houses, not only did he abandon caves, but these curious, mysterious openings into the earth took on a sinister aspect. Home to bats, silent creatures of the night, caves became enmeshed in legends in which they were seen as entrances to a dangerous underworld, perhaps even a gateway into hell itself.

Not until the 18th century did scientists begin exploring caves, albeit at first in a limited way, as lighting was difficult. Their reward was the discovery of the bones of extinct animals, which were claimed to prove that Noah's Flood really did happen.

Although scientific interest in the seas had begun as early as the 18th century, when Count Luigi Marsigli made observations of the salinity, temperature and currents of the Mediterranean, it was the spread of submarine telegraphy in the 19th century which really stimulated a need to understand the waves and currents of the deep sea floor. This coupled, with the publication of Darwin's *Origin of Species*, which sparked interest in marine biology, led to the voyage of HMS *Challenger*, which in 1872 set out on a three-year voyage, marking the birth of modern oceanography. Although human exploration of shallow waters was possible through diving, the true depths remained uncharted until the development in 1930 of a vessel strong enough to protect explorers from the immense pressure at the ocean floor – the bathysphere.

limits brought the death of one of their team, Maurice Fargues, who reached 120 m (396 ft) before they lost touch with him, later finding him with his mouthpiece dangling at his chest. Despite this tragic loss, the Aqua-Lung had set the standard for future diving systems.

After the war, and during the time that Piccard was developing the *Trieste*, Cousteau, frustrated with the limits of scuba diving, was approaching deep-sea exploration craft from a different angle. Although the bathyscaphe had proved its ability to reach the deepest of depths, its weight and design meant that it lacked the power of manoeuvrability, something which the true exploration of the undersea world vitally required. Cousteau, whilst on board his ship *Calypso* on the Red Sea, began to shape his ideas for a new deep-sea diving craft.

With his prerequisites being that it needed to be light enough to carry on Calypso, and that it needed to carry two people, Cousteau came up with the shape of a flattened ball for this new craft. It was to move like 'angels' he said, the way his Aqua-Lung had allowed divers to move, and it also made use of the lessons learned in the building of the bathyscaphe. The new vehicle, the 3-metre long (nine-foot) *Soucoupe* weighed just four tons, its pilots lay on their stomachs to peer out of larger windows: it had cameras and lights attached and it had a claw to collect specimens. Soucoupe became the prototype of all modern undersea research vehicles and was capable of withstanding pressures that conventional submarines would have collapsed under. The *Soucoupe* began diving in 1959 and was in service for over three decades.

Index

DATE 11-22-2015 3:07PM
Item(s) checked out to p. 986769

TITLE: No good men... red line no...
BRCD: 30041005214000
DUE DATE: 12-13 15

TITLE: The mysterious death of Mr. Books...
BRCD: 30041001713577
DUE DATE: 12-13 15

TITLE: The last train from Hiroshima : t
BRCD: 30041003944746